NEVER GIVE UP

NEVER GIVE UP

Terry Brennan

Copyright © 2024 Terry Brennan

The moral right of the author has been asserted.

Apart from any fair dealing for the purposes of research or private study, or criticism or review, as permitted under the Copyright, Designs and Patents Act 1988, this publication may only be reproduced, stored or transmitted, in any form or by any means, with the prior permission in writing of the publishers, or in the case of reprographic reproduction in accordance with the terms of licences issued by the Copyright Licensing Agency. Enquiries concerning reproduction outside those terms should be sent to the publishers.

Troubador Publishing Ltd
Unit E2 Airfield Business Park
Harrison Road, Market Harborough
Leicestershire LE16 7UL
Tel: 0116 279 2299
Email: books@troubador.co.uk
Web: www.troubador.co.uk

ISBN 978-1-80514-352-9

British Library Cataloguing in Publication Data.
A catalogue record for this book is available from the British Library.

Printed and bound in Great Britain by CMP UK
Typeset in 11pt Minion Pro by Troubador Publishing Ltd, Leicester, UK

DEDICATED

To my sister Sheila

Contents

	Acknowledgments	ix
1	The Orphanage	1
2	Holidays	4
3	Growing up	7
4	A Sister	10
5	A New Life	12
6	The Solicitor's Office	19
7	The Call Up	21
8	The Wedding	33
9	A Move to the East End	36
10	My Changing	42
11	The Running club	47
12	A Holiday in Sweden	49
13	The Church in Leyton	51
14	Suspicion	54
15	Barbara, my new partner	57
16	Lucy	64
17	Ireland	69
18	Dean and Jackie's wedding	73

19	John's wedding	75
20	Back in Dumfries	77
21	Neil's wedding	79
22	Return to Ireland	82
23	A Heart Attack	85
24	Mandy's Wedding in London	87
25	The DNA results	89
26	Trips to London	94
27	Meeting the Nieces	97
28	Back in Dumfries	101
29	Another Trip to London	104
30	Terry's Story	108
	The Family Tree	110

Acknowledgements

Where do I start for there are so many to thank? They appear here in no order of merit for all are of equal importance to this story.

Many thanks to our specialist Michelle Leonard, without whose help we would never have solved the many mysteries we were confronted with. And Per Halvorsen whose dedication, inspiration, and friendship have shown me the ways of genealogy, I am indebted to you both.

To my sister, Sheila, who has journeyed with me and been my constant support. To my son Stephen and Neil my nephew, who both have urged me to create this story. I would like to also thank my newfound nieces Margaret, Teresa, Debby, and Anita Bedford for the small bits of information to add to what we found about our family. To Barbara, my loving partner.

Finally, to author Miller Caldwell who has edited and helped put this story together, and to all the family people whom I've met and built my life around a huge thank you.

1

The Orphanage

In 1939 Terry Brennan was placed in the care of a woman who, in later years, was the only person to have known his mother as they both lived in the same London area. This lady was responsible for him being sent to an orphanage in Kent. It was an orphanage run by the London County Council for the benefit of children who were evacuated during the Second World War and for children with no apparent parents. There were both boys and girls housed in care, but they lived separately.

Terry was placed in the nursery being in the three years to five age group. His mother could not look after him and so like many other children, was put into care in an orphanage.

His registration number was 6739 in area 3 and he was admitted on 21st March 1944 with a date of birth noted as 7th

February 1939, born in St George's Hospital in East Wapping, London, according to the London County Council records supplied by the woman who had placed him in care.

Being so young, he was placed in the nursery in St Annes in the girl's area where new babies and the very young were cared for and kept until they were 6 years old. That was when he was moved to the main boy's section in St Josephs. Being classed as an orphan and illegitimate, he was under the Poor Law Act of 1930, section 154 paragraph 1 (f), and homed in St Annes.

The details held on his behalf recorded his parents as being Patrick Brennan and Bridget Brennan. It was assumed that they were the friends of Mrs. Winters in the years prior to him going into the orphanage.

The vast building was in fact two schools, one for each sex with a huge church between the two schools and the community was largely self-sufficient with a farm, an infirmary, a carpenter's room, a bakery shop, a shoe repair shop and a sweet shop. There were also three playing fields and two very large fields for cultivating crops of potatoes, cabbage and wheat. A gymnasium, allotments and a library were there too. The dormitories were huge with fifty boys sleeping in three sections according to age.

After his 6th birthday he was moved once more. He was now in a room of boys his own age and for the first time he had to wear a uniform so they all looked the same, except for the expressions on their faces. Some boys were delighted to have visits from relations but for Terry and many like him, there were no visits. It was upsetting. He remembers he cried a lot at first.

Biggin Hill airport was not far away. Planes setting off for Germany flew over the school. The children waved at them. But they also heard Doodlebugs over their heads and when they fell silent, there followed a huge explosion. When they were flying around, they had to run to the air shelters or lay flat on the ground until it was safe to come out.

In the air-shelter, there were rows of canvas bunks with a very low wattage light. Terry was on the top bunk, near the door. One night he was bored and decided to spit at a stone on the floor for no reason, but he reached out too far. He fell headlong to the floor hitting his head on the concrete surface and screamed. The senior in charge sought help from the office and as a result, he was rushed to Orpington Hospital not far away.

The fall was so serious that he was in hospital for a few weeks for treatment, after which he was transferred to Farnborough, still in Kent, together with his identity card and a clothing ration book. When he was finally better, he was transferred to Hesketh Bank in Lancashire.

He had a great time playing in pools of water splattered with mud, within a barrack-type perimeter. Terry admits to having great fun there. When the war was over, he returned to Orpington where he lived with the juniors and moved to a new dormitory. There, he mixed well with the other boys and was given pocket money for sweets in the shop. He recalls he could have a large selection of sweets in a paper bag for thruppence. However, if he was naughty, the pocket money would be withdrawn.

2

Holidays

Terry is above the cross on the bottom row.

Every year they were taken on holiday to Dymchurch in Kent. It was a tented campsite. There were bell tents which slept three boys and there was a huge Marquee used as a dining room. The site also had a washroom and a shower room. The camp was near a miniature Railway called the Dymchurch Line and it ran from Folkstone to Rhye along the Kent coast. The rail embankment ran along the top edge of the campsite.

One day they were all lined up and questioned about a break-in at the tuck shop outside the camp. The staff were keen to find the culprit. Eventually, they found him. A senior boy. He'd broken into the shop during the night and hidden his cache by burying the sweets on the railway embankment. But he could not find where he had hidden his booty, so he was placed in confinement until the boys returned to Orpington. He was then sent to a borstal for his offence.

Despite this incident, Terry loved Dymchurch holidays as he was able to swim in the sea and sit on the beach. He went there for several years, but one year they went to the Isle of Wight at Sandown where a similar campsite with bell tents was found.

Here he saw the Spithead Review, a Coronation review of over 300 ships British naval ships as they sailed through the channel. It was a great sight to see as he lined up on the grassy bank and it was a sight he would never forget.

Back at school in Orpington, Terry was given the chance to join the Boy Scouts. Not every boy thought it a good idea, but Terry was keen to join. The Scouts headquarters were at Petts Wood, just three stops along the line from Orpington. Six boys took the train once a month to the scout hut. There he learned to read maps and was set on an orientation walk by being dropped off a mile away and instructed to find their way home, although they knew they were being watched by staff to ensure they did not get lost).

As a scout, he also ventured to the Chislehurst caves as well as a trip to the Mendip hills. Terry realised being a scout was a great steppingstone in his life, preparing for when he eventually left school.

As a growing pupil, he was allowed to go to the Orpington pictures, but they rarely paid. One of the boys was put through a toilet window and would get them into the picture house by the back door. The ice cream lady knew what they were doing but took pity on them and never told her superiors how the boys entered the picture house.

One quiet night in the dormitory, Terry decided to go to the allotment with his pillowcase and get some carrots. When all was quiet, he made for the stair fire escape onto the swimming pool roof and down the clinging ivy to the allotments. He gathered what he could and returned to his room. But as he entered, he was confronted by a staff member. He was taken to the gymnasium that same night at 9p.m. and a cane whacked his backside and then more strokes on his hands.

It was a painful episode.

Terry, on the right.

3

Growing Up

As a 10-year-old and now in a second-form class, he was taught to read Latin and had to recite it to his teacher, so he knew he was able to follow the mass in church. He was chosen to serve the priest at the altar and respond to him during the service as he had learned Latin by heart. On Sundays, the girl's school sat on the left aisle while the boys sat on the right, ready to assist in serving at the mass. At times, Terry felt he was being prepared for the priesthood. He attended the Benediction too, and at the occasional funeral which the priest conducted. Terry was even made to rise at 6a.m. to serve at the priest's private chapel, long before breakfast. He felt his day was being dominated by religion and he resented that.

At the age of 12, he moved to the senior boys and was allowed to play football. But to get to the pitch, they had to form a line to walk along the street and sometimes to the railway station and back, looking like a column of prisoners. They were not allowed to play near the embankment where fast trains sped by from London heading for the coast. He recalls seeing the Golden Arrow, a famous steam train, bellow its smoke along the way with sparks flying from its wheels.

On one particularly hot day, the sparks shot up and lit the dry grass embankment setting it alight. Soon the whole embankment was on fire and the fire brigade was summoned but it took them some time to extinguish the flames and dampen the heat. Terry saw the whole operation and for a moment wondered if he could be a fireman.

There was a play yard at the school and they played hockey and skittles there. They also set three sticks against the wall and threw the ball at them. There was a wall in front of the bakery and a lower wall at one end of the playground, where one could stand on someone else's back, get over the wall and run to the fields. With the teacher being absorbed in his prayer ritual, it gave them a chance to escape. One day, Terry was at the end of the playground where the bread was being sliced in the machine slicer. The window was always slightly open. If you raised the window quietly a hand could find the goodies. The boys were always hungry. But as Terry grabbed the freshly baked warm bread, he was seen by Brother Paul, a plump little man who lifted his habit, tucked it into his belt and chased after him. He was far behind Terry though, so he jumped over a fence and lay flat as he could but as Brother Paul ran past him, he noticed him. There and then, he was nabbed by the priest and marched back to face the music.

It was not music Terry heard nor felt at 9p.m. that evening as he was marched to the gymnasium, but he was not the only boy in attendance. They were lined up in 3 lines and the brother produced his cane which he warmed up as he beat it lightly against his cloak. He called the first boy's name out. He held his crossed hands out and received three almighty strokes. Then the next boy received the same punishment and so on until all had received their three strokes. But the brother had not finished. The punishment for more serious offences was then addressed, where all the boys were made to observe the next torturous episode, including those who had already been punished. The more serious offenders, still recovering from their hand-warming pain, lifted their nightgowns to reveal bare buttocks which were then given three whacks to each boy. Embossed lines on the buttocks made sitting and sleeping uncomfortable for a few days.

Some lesser offences such as being late for a school class, having a hole in your trousers, losing your handkerchief, in fact any little thing they could detect, resulted in losing some pocket money. The pupils were given 1/6p on Saturday but that could be reduced to 1/- or even less to spend in the sweet shop.

There were 6 classrooms and he was now in the top senior class with Brother Cartridge, who he thought was an excellent teacher. He noticed Terry had a good style of writing and took him aside to inform him that there was a competition for boys in the local paper, (the children were not allowed newspapers, local or national). Brother Cartridge told Terry he would send one of his essays to the paper and he did. A week or so later he informed him he had won but Terry never received any acknowledgment of his effort in any form or found out exactly what it was he had "won". This naturally upset him. Despite being a good teacher, Brother Cartridge could be cruel. He had a spaniel dog called Roger. Onde day, he decided to cut off its tail and place it in the gutter outside of the classroom. They decided to report him to the headmaster, but nothing became of it.

The headmaster always had the best interests of his pupils in mind. He cared for their future. He gave Terry the opportunity to look after 500 chickens, cleaning their hutches every day and gathering their eggs. He had to make them tightly secure at night as some had been killed by rats which were rife under the hutches. At this farm there were three horses. Terry particularly loved the one called Bonnie Prince Charlie, but he was learning to plough the fields with one of the others named Mernuagh who was the same age as him. Above all else, Terry enjoyed riding the cart to the fields.

4
A Sister

One morning while in the playground, Terry was called unexpectedly into the headmaster's office. This usually meant you were in trouble so, of course, he thought this was the case, but he could not think for what. His heart was in his mouth as he arrived at the headmaster's door. He was asked to take a seat in his study. This was a most unfamiliar setting.

He informed him that a Mr. Clark from the LCC (London County Council) was here to speak to him. He had brought some papers with him. 'I have some news for you,' said the headmaster. 'Are you ready for this?'

He found no words to say but nodded to show he understood what he was saying so far.

'Mr. Clark has asked me to inform you that you have a sister in the school next door and her name is Sheila Brennan. We have proof that she is your sister, and you are going to meet her today in St Anne's.'

His mouth was slightly open. Perhaps a smile would have been more appropriate, but he had never had a family member visit him over the years and he was even unsure if this girl, Sheila, would be his sister. Yet he had no reason to doubt the headmaster or Mr. Clark.

He was taken to St Anne's to meet the head nun. In her office sat a girl. She stood up as the nun said, 'Terry, this is your sister, Sheila.'

They nodded at each other without a word. Then Terry smiled at her, and her lips parted ever so slightly in a shallow smile. 'Hello,' he said, and she responded likewise.

They were encouraged to sit down and talk. Terry told her where he had been over his growing years, and she did likewise. He told her where he would be working the following year when he was 15. He suggested they meet each Sunday, and go to the swings in her playground. They couldn't help speaking at the same time such was their interest in finding out about each other. The nun said she would arrange for him to visit on Sunday afternoons and stay for tea. He smiled at her. It seemed Sheila had a thoughtful head nun.

In his final year at the orphanage, he worked in the potato field, packing them up in sacks and placing them on the cart which the horse took to the farm for storage, for use in the kitchen.

Eventually the news came that he was about to leave school. He was given some new clothes and an envelope containing his personal life history with the LCC. He was told he would be staying with a family in Surrey and Mr. Clark would be taking him there in two weeks' time, the day after his 15th birthday.

5
—
A New Life

When Terry was 15 years of age, Mr. Clark accompanied him from Orpington station to Victoria, then on to another train to New Malden in Surrey to stay with Mrs. Freeman and her husband and daughter at a house in Cavendish Road. He was to lodge with them until he was 18 years of age. They were foster parents, provided by the LCC. They were good substitute parents and, of course, religious. That meant regular church attendance continued and he had his own room but after a settling-in period, he needed to get a job.

He attended the Labour Exchange seeking any job they thought suitable for him. They had a position. It was at the local Co-op, so he was sent along to be interviewed by the manager. It was a perfunctory interview after which he told him he would start on Monday.

He was thrilled to have his first job. He worked inside at the back of the Co-op, packing shelves with provisions and was asked to do various tasks by the regular staff. He had to get two buses to get to work but Mr. Freeman (Colin) and his wife helped him to get around New Malden. Soon he was a man of the world, visiting places like Kingston and Hampton Court on his days off.

His room wasn't a large one so he couldn't fill it much with anything other than his clothes. Mrs. Freeman was a good cook, and he began to put on a little weight. Colin was a post office engineer and could fix anything with his hands. He impressed him. Terry got on well with him.

Next door was a family of three boys (Joseph, Ben, and Brian) and their mum, Mrs. Hellings. They would ask him to go with them to local cafes but they also asked him if he'd like to go to a live jazz club one day. It only cost a shilling to get in and when they went, Terry found he loved it when they played traditional jazz. One band were particularly good. It was Ken Colyer's group. They were fabulous, which led him to buy their records. In those days, cafes had jukeboxes and he always selected jazz records. Working at the Co-op, he was earning more money than he ever had, so he saved some and eventually bought a bike, as the three boys had bikes too. It was a Holdsworth Racing bike and as he got used to it, he was keen to work up speed and keep up with the boys as they visited nearby towns such as Morden and Guildford and many other places.

At the Co-op, Terry was asked to report to the manager's office one day and asked if he'd like to slice bacon. That meant going twice a week to be trained in the art of bacon slicing at Woolwich RACS, the main store. He passed the test and returned to the Co-op a fully trained Bacon Cutter which almost doubled his pay.

While staying with the Freemans, Terry met a girl who was perhaps his first love interest. Her name was Lorna Wollard and she lived in Worcester Park, not far from the Freemans. They went out a bit to cafés and jazz clubs, but he was still very shy with girls, and he never kissed her. It was just a friendship, and he was scared, if the truth be known, to kiss her. In time they parted, and her parents seemed slightly upset as they seemed to like him.

Terry was now seventeen, but his days as a seventeen-year-old were soon to end and that meant a severing from the LCC and his placement with the Freeman family. He was not upset at leaving the Freeman household as he was determined to find his own abode. He found lodgings in a house quite near the Co-op. The landlady there had also found a second lodger who was three years older than himself, which he didn't mind as it meant it was cheaper. They got on well and did their own thing. He was a bit crippled, so he had a simple job, but he did own an Austin car which was very old. Terry was told his mother had left it to him, so he assumed she had died as she never came to visit, and he never spoke of her. He never had a licence and his handicap meant he couldn't drive the car anyway, so he would sit in it, start the engine and rev it up. The car never left the drive.

Terry always kept in touch with Sheila especially to find out where she would be after leaving school. He had found his sister and he never wanted to lose her. She was his only family and he suspected she felt the same way about him.

One day he took a day off work and went to see the lady who had taken him in when he was at school twice at weekends for respite, as the saying went. He suspected the staff had the weekend off on these occasions. He went because he thought she had taken ill. Her son Michael was the boy who had helped him to learn more about history. They used to sit and talk about the past. He recalled the time when a boy called Bernard, who was with them at school, was on a trolley bus and he got up to leave the bus as he thought it was his stop. But the bus was going too fast and Bernard jumped off and crashed to the ground. He smashed his head rather badly. The driver saw what had happened in his mirror and stopped the trolleybus. He rang for an ambulance and Bernard was rushed to hospital with lights flashing. When Terry got back to school, he remembers he was asked to give the Head Priest a report of the incident. Michael had often wondered what had happened to him. So did Terry.

One day, he decided to go to Somerset House where all the records for Births, Deaths and Marriages are kept, to see if he could find out more about his own history. He took all his documentation with him, especially the envelope which Mr. Clark gave him when he left school. It cost him 7 shillings and he had to wait for an attendant to see him and assist in his search, but it was all in vain. There was no record of his birth, despite the attendant sifting through all the papers that he had in the envelope, including an identity card signed by Bridget Brennan. The attendant told Terry that he could find no trace of his mother.

The letter from Mrs. Winters was as follows.

Mrs. Winters lived at 10 Southern Street Islington. She had been a friend of Bridget Brennan in 1939 and some years before that date. Bridget told her that Terry was sent to Oak Hall Nursery 24th March 1943 and then to St Francis Nursery at Bala on 28th January 1944 and then on 1st March 1945 to St Anne's Orpington, Kent. It was noted that Terry was born in St George's the East Hospital workhouse in Poplar, London. It was recorded that his mother was married to a Mr. Patrick Brennan in Kilkenny and he was born on 12th October 1900. Bridget's date of birth was 6th March 1902 and she died at Lamberth Hospital on 3rd March 1943. The letter showed Sheila was born 23rd January 1942 and was boarded out on 15th September 1942 as an eight-month baby to Goldburne Rd Nursery in Berkshire. The document also showed his mother had lived at 178 Caledonian Road Islington N1 London. There was also a baptismal certificate that was registered at Our Lady's Hospital in Surrey showing

Terry was the son of Patrick and Bridget Brennan. But a question mark over the date of Terry's birth noted it was 7th February 1939.

Even with this documentation, the clerks at Somerset House were unable to trace Terry's birth. Not having a Birth Certificate or anyway to prove who he was, Terry would find it almost impossible to obtain a passport. But he did return to Somerset House and found Sheila's birth certificate dated 23rd January 1942. He sent that to her when he found out her new address.

On Sheila's certificate, it said the same as on his. Sheila was registered on 1st May 1947 and the father was a greengrocer, in the markets of London, so the link between Sheila and Terry was that they had the same parents. This was then a starting block for him to delve more into his family history.

Terry used to cycle around to Brian's house and set off with the boys to the pub by the station. They usually drank Scrumpy, which was strong, and he couldn't drink more than two pints. A couple of times he got drunk, was sick and then staggered home. It seemed that was part of growing up!

Terry's work was going well, so he often fed himself in the cafés and bought new clothes. His wages had again increased as he was not only a qualified bacon cutter, but he was also cooking York Hams in the huge steam cooker. It could cook at least 20 gammon joints and form them into hams for slicing. He would walk into the fridges where the hams lay, and place them on trays ready for the shop aisles. He seemed to be a natural butcher and the manager was pleased with his work ethic.

Then one day a letter arrived from the Home Office, requesting his presence. He showed it to his manager, and the manager gave him the day off.

Terry arrived in good time at this large, impressive building. A man appeared and asked him into his room. He asked for his papers which he had thankfully brought, and he asked him what other information he could tell him. The man sat studying them for a while and occasionally peppered him with questions as he read about Terry's life. He took a copy of Terry's papers from a copier in the room, and as he returned to his desk, he informed Terry that he would contact him, and told him that before he did anything else, he should wait until he heard from him.

A few days later he received a registered letter, which reads as follows:

With reference to your visit on 9th April, I am writing to explain from the details supplied by you, we have made a search in our records for an entrance of birth relating to Terance Brennan born on 7th February 1939 at Lambeth Hospital, but the search has proved unsuccessful and therefore appears that your birth was not registered, and escaped registration. As explained to you during your recent visit here, after the expiration of 12 months from the date of birth, the registration of the birth can be effected only if this is authorized by the Registrar General and upon attendance of a duly qualified person at a registered office to give information for the registration, and moreover, before the Registrar General can authorize the registration of the birth, he must be satisfied by documentary evidence as to the precise date and place of birth. As it would appear that the above conditions cannot now be fulfilled, it is regretted that the late registration of birth cannot be authorized. In the circumstances, you may wish to consider making a statutory declaration before a Justice of the Peace, a Magistrate, A Commissioner For Oaths, or a practicing solicitor, setting out the date and place of birth and the parent's names, and including a statement that to the best of your knowledge and belief, your birth has not been registered, and such a declaration if made, should not be sent here but should be retained by yourself and produced in lieu of a birth certificate whenever evidence of your age and identity is required. A form for this purpose of the declaration is not supplied by this office but by a law stationer.

Now he knew what he had to do to prove who he was before he could obtain a passport and be able to legally declare he was English and a British subject.

6

The Solicitor's Office

His next step was to phone Mr. Clark at the LCC office for advice on where to go next. He recommended Terry go to Lincoln's Inn Fields in Holborn and speak to someone there. He did exactly that and a man agreed to investigate his case. He had to swear an oath that the evidence he had given was the truth as far as he was aware, and it was accepted. He was also told to go to the Home Office again. Spurred on, he did so and about four days later he received this reply:

> *In reply to your letter dated 31st July 1979, I am directed by the Secretary of State to inform you that nationality is a matter of law that can be determined conclusively only by the courts. Nevertheless, on the basis of such information and documentary evidence as you have been able to furnish, the Secretary of State is prepared for his part to regard you as a British citizen of the United Kingdom and Colonies under section 12(1) of the British Nationality Act of 1948, and consequently, a British subject can now apply for a passport if required.*

Terry was so pleased with this result and kept all his papers in a new strong folder. He lost no time in going to the Passport Office, paid the required fee, and returned to work as happy as Larry. He had a few weeks to wait before his passport would arrive. But that was no time at all.

The letter duly arrived but once again, it was a big setback. The letter read:

I refer to your application for a British passport. We regret to inform you that as you are unable to produce a birth certificate, we cannot proceed with your request. We advise you to contact the Home Office. They should contact us and inform us they have approved your evidence, then we could consider your application again for a passport.

He did that of course but wondered as he was a taxpayer, why he could not get a passport, as he was registered to pay tax on his wages. It seemed so unfair. There seemed to be so many difficulties set in his way.

He kept up his communication with Sheila telling her about all the offices and departments of the State he had been meeting. She sympathized with his efforts and hoped they would eventually give him the answers he needed.

7

The Call Up

Terry was at work one day and the day had started well. The Co-op manager had informed him that the store was going to have a special offer on bacon products. This of course meant overtime to get the trays of sliced bacon, corned beef, and ham ready, So he would earn some extra cash. There was a skip to his step going home that week, but it was too good to last. When he got home, the landlady informed him he had an important official letter. He opened it and his heart missed a beat. He had to report to Euston station the following Monday for National Service. This meant the army for Terry, but how was he going to show his birth certificate? He realised he had to report to the station though. It was the law after all.

He sold his bike, gave in his notice to the Co-op manager who told him a position would always be there for him, said goodbye to the Freeman family, had a Thursday night pub meeting with the Co-op staff and said his goodbyes to everyone he knew. Sheila wished him luck and good fortune.

Monday morning came and at Euston station, he met the fierce-sounding sergeant. It transpired he was about to board a train to Ballymena in Northern Ireland! He wondered why he was being sent there, after all, he was a Londoner, that was undeniable. The only connection was his surname. Yes of course, he was half Irish too, as Bridget and Patrick Brennan came from the Emerald Isle, but his fellow soldiers had all sorts of British accents. It was a long train journey stopping eventually at Stranraer on the Southwest coast of Scotland. There they boarded a ferry to Belfast. And on to Ballymena Barracks where he learned he was to join the Royal Ulster Rifles. But he wasn't a soldier yet. For six weeks he learned to keep his uniform and kit clean, with Blanco, Brasso and hard work. One recruit who was ill-suited to army life spread Blanco on his bedsheets and blankets hoping he would be dismissed from the army. But he was put in 'jankers' – denied privileges for the day then made to wash off the Blanco from his bedding and warned if he did anything like that again, he would be severely reprimanded. The training was harsh and as Terry was only 5ft 4 inches tall, he was always in the middle of the line on parade. They marched at 144 paces per minute, and he had a job keeping up, but he soon got used to the 5-mile marches. However, the march across the Mountains of Mourne was more of a slog.

The sergeant and corporals in charge of the squad, Gallipoli, Whittaker, and Redmond, were very strict with us and made them work hard.

Although their rifles only carried blanks at this point, they had to carry them all the time outside the barracks. He got used to the weight and feel of the rifle and in due course, was later supplied with live ammunition.

Each day the guard changed so it meant they lined up as 8 men on the square in two rows and were inspected by the captain of the day. He would choose the best turned out man to march to the end of the square and appoint him as Stick of the Day. That meant he was the CO's (Commanding Officer) runner of the day but also meant he'd get off guard duty and be provided extra pay that week. So, it paid to polish your boots till your face shined in the toes and have your kit well Blanco smeared.

As the weeks rolled on, they were tested in education classes which meant Terry was suited, by virtue of his years as a scout, to be good at map reading. So, he volunteered to do reconnaissance. It meant riding on a Saracen tank where he directed the driver with his map-reading skills in the open fields of Antrim. Terry loved his work as at times, it got him off marching. It was a specialized job, and he was one of only four men taken from different squads to ride the Saracens.

When they had completed their basic training, they were posted to Germany at Iserlohn barracks, near Dusseldorf, not too far from the Black Forest, some 50 miles away on the autobahn. The area was full of trees and open ground for the use of exercises. At times, in this lush area, would be 'battles' with other regiments. On another occasion, the test was to get to Cologne Cathedral, about 20 miles away, without being spotted by the scout cars who were on the road. On one occasion when Terry detected a scout car, he jumped over a hedge and landed on a huge cow pat and was up to his knees in dung. Fortunately, there was a cow's water trough nearby and he was able to clean himself as best he could. He then carried on his way, reaching the Cathedral where he entered and collected a few pamphlets as proof he had succeeded in reaching his target. All the men were gathered and collected and taken back to barracks where points were awarded for being successful and points meant pounds, or in this case, Deutsche Marks!

Later that day in the dining room, Terry spotted a man. He seemed to know him. The man told him he did not know Terry, but they shared a table anyway and he got to know him a little bit better. He was a Londoner. He had the crooked nose of a boxer from his many fights over the years. He had served his time in Cyprus during the EOKA terrorist period and told Terry about the dangerous missions he'd been on. Thankfully, that skirmish in Cyprus had ended and the regiment had been brought back to Iserlohn where Terry was stationed. But he was about to be de-mobbed so they said they would write to each other, but it never happened.

Terry's training continued, including going to large rifle ranges for practice at long-range targets. These were long and tiring days, especially as the soldiers had to march and shoot at the same time, so his favourite time remained riding on the Saracen tanks. On one occasion, they were moved out early from a starting point in the open forest where Terry was ready and waiting for his call over the radio to move to a specific point. When it was safe for them to do so, the foot soldiers would cross the bridge on the Saracens' instruction, and then report back to headquarters. At 4 a.m. the exercise began. Off they went in search of any hidden enemy soldiers and once captured, they had to ensure they had proof of their capture.

But they were not doing exercises every day. The men were given some time off. When they were free, they left the barracks wearing civvies and entered the pubs. The Oktoberfest brought back happy memories of his time before the army, but the beer was strong and made many sick or drunk. If the men returned to camp and were still under the influence of alcohol in the morning parade, it led to a big fine, So they had to be careful. Terry used to go to the jazz clubs in the local town to see the Dutch Swing College Band. They were fantastic and Terry still has some of their records to this day. Then came a real dilemma. Terry was offered a promotion to be a lance corporal. But he wished to stay on as a rifleman and steered away from the additional responsibility.

While in the army he kept in touch with his sister Sheila and was pleased to hear how she had followed his footsteps and was now in the Women's Royal Army Corp regiment, in Shropshire.

Terry learned that she had found a boyfriend from Scotland, Boyd Carmichael. He was pleased for them. Terry was not so lucky in love. He had dated one sort of girlfriend in Germany, but it did not come to anything, especially as there was a language difficulty. Terry had completed two and a half years in the army and was asked to sign on for another three years. He informed his commanding officer that he would be willing to spend another year in the forces and that meant two things. A rise in pay and a new status. He was now a regular soldier.

The extra year flew by. He did a lot more map reading to avoid parades but sometimes had to do guard duty. The thought that him standing at the back entrance of the barracks at 5' 4" would not stop an intruder from pushing him over and walking straight into the camp, passed his mind, but Germany was now a peaceful country and experienced no internal or external threat.

His last job before returning to Ballymena was as a Batman to an officer. He spent a couple of months as his valet and drove the officer's car around the barracks in first gear. It was the first time he had ever driven a car, but fortunately no one noticed.

The day came for him to pack up his kit and the jazz records he had acquired and leave Germany. The plane took Terry to Manchester and from there, on to a train to Stranraer and a boat to Belfast. The boat was much slower and gave him time to prepare for his final tour in Ulster. More guard duty was to follow. This time at Stormont Castle where dignitaries, politicians, and foreign guests arrived. All were saluted by Terry when he not carrying his rifle, but he presented arms when he had his arms to present. He got jobs in the officer's mess. He would wait for instruction from other officers and wash up their cutlery and dishes. It was during this soporific soapy chore his life was to change once more. One day, an officer came for a drink of water.

'Good morning, Brennan. How are you today? Looking

forward to your release in a few weeks?' he asked as the water filled his glass.

'Good morning, sir. I can't wait to leave now the time is getting nearer.'

'Where will you be going? Where will you stay?' the officer enquired.

'I've nowhere to go to specifically. But I'll find something.'

Later that day, Terry brought out his personal envelope and showed the officer the letter from Mrs. Winter. He studied it with care and interest.

'Do you mind if I hold on to this for a while? I'd like to read this fully. I'll return it to you later, Brennan.'

He saluted him and turned to leave his room.

'One moment Brennan.' Said the officer. 'I'm putting you on C.O. orders in the morning. Come and see me then.'

The next morning, he marched into his room to be at his disposal. But the officers words invited him to sit down. He told him to go on four days' leave to London and visit Mrs. Winters and see if she could help find a place for him to live. Terry was to report back to him in five days' time.

Terry set off early the next day in his civvies. He got to Euston early in the afternoon. He asked at the station how far away was Southern Street, off Caledonian Road and was told it was within walking distance. He soon found the address, Number 10.

He stood in silence at first. What reception would he get if she was still at this property? He knocked on the door. And a little old woman opened the door and asked what he wanted, and when Terry mentioned his name, Mrs. Winters immediately reacted. She screamed upstairs, calling someone to come down quickly and see who it was at the door, dragging him inside into the front room as she did. When her daughter Liz came in and she explained who this was, Liz could not believe her mother had put Terry in an orphanage in 1944 while still being the friend of Terry's mother. They asked about Sheila and Terry was quick to tell them they had been in touch for a few years now and she was in the Women's Army. He told them his pressing need was to find somewhere to stay when he left the army in a couple of weeks.

Liz said that her sister Mary round the corner could put him up and she said she'd take him around to see her immediately. (Mrs. Winters had 9 grown-up children. Six were still alive namely Charlie, Liz, Mary, Ann, and John.) Liz took Terry around to seen Mary, but she had little idea who Terry was. Mary was very tall. She was a six-footer and had a teenage daughter who was also called Mary.

Terry suspected he was suffering from shock having uncovered such a large local family but one thing for sure was that he would soon have a home to go to.

When Terry got back to Ballymena, he sought out the Commanding Officer in his office, but he was not there. Instead, he was in the mess and when he heard of Terry's success in obtaining lodgings in London, he was elated to learn that he would be staying with this family.

Terry on a Saracen scout vehicle.

His demobilization day arrived. He was given the credits he'd earned, a favorable report signed by the C.O. and his release documents. He was allowed to retain his army bonnets and cap badges as a momentum of his time in the army, and a train ticket to London was provided. So, his army days were truly over. He had learned an awful lot and had had a great time in Germany and Ireland. His journey home was full of expectations. Young Mary met him at the station and helped carry his stuff and got him to her home where they made him feel welcome and Terry settled in immediately.

Mrs. Winter could always be found in the pub along the road near King's Cross station called the Queens. It was a dingy old pub but that is what she liked, and it wasn't too far for her to walk home, so he used to go along and have a drink with her. She loved her bottle of Guinness as well as snuff. She would sniff it from the back of her hand up her nose and as such, her handkerchief was always brown coloured. They got on well, but although she spoke fondly of Terry's mother and recalled him as a very young child and Sheila being born, she said very little else. Terry managed to find out that Mrs. Winter had taken responsibility for his mother's funeral and that she was buried in a cemetery in East Finchley, but she had not attended the burial as it was a pauper's funeral in which 15 people would rest in the same grave.

Terry contacted Sheila to tell her what he had found out about their mother. Sheila informed him she had left the army and had moved with Boyd to live on a Scottish farm, near his parents in Ayrshire. He was pleased that she now had a home and one that he'd hope to try to visit sometime. He told her about Mrs. Winter's recollections and the cemetery, but as things turned out, it was young Mary who recommended Terry should go to the council offices if he wished to find out more, which he decided he would do.

There, he was given a map of the cemetery, a number and a plot. He was to expect that as she was 1 of 15 interred, it would be hard to find it as it would probably be overgrown. But he'd give it a try.

On the day, he set out on the bus and found the gates of the cemetery on the map. It seemed a very long walk down the plot, but he found the site. It was up a slight embankment partly hidden by trees. He looked around and found small discs with numbers in a small area. He found the number he had been given, 23411. He cleared the area of tree branches, overgrown weeds, and nettles and stacked them on a small pathway edge to the left. So, this is where his mother, Bridget Brennan was buried with 15 other people. It was a sad place, especially to think of them all being paupers, but at least they were at peace together. He made a promise to himself that he would make a point to come and keep her grave tidy. He contacted Sheila and informed her that he had found their mother's grave and she was really pleased. She would meet him and go with him to the grave next time she was in London.

As ever money was a problem, so Terry searched for work in the area where he was now living. The Employment office recommended him for a job in a wallpaper warehouse on Offord Road, off Caledonian Rd, which would mean only a short walk to work. After an interview, he got the work as a warehouseman and that meant making up bundles of wallpaper for the 20 or so shops, they owned around London. Blakely Morris was the name of the company.

With regular money coming in, he was able to pay his way in the house but there was another problem. Mary was an office worker in the city. That meant an early start for her. The problem was there was no indoor bathroom, and the toilet was outside. So, it meant Terry clashed with her at times in the morning while she washed in the sink in the kitchen and of course, she required her privacy in the outside toilet. The problem was solved with Terry staying in his bed longer and waiting for her to leave the house.

In due course, he met the extended family. Charlie was around 60 years of age and lived in the King's Cross area; Annie also lived nearby, with her husband George and they had a son, Michael. John lived with his mother Nelly Winters around the corner and Tom lived in Holborn with his wife and two children. Terry was welcomed into this expanded family and was treated as one of them. He found it good to be amongst these streetwise market stall traders and he enjoyed meeting them in the pub after work.

Then one day the sad news of the death of 12-year-old Michael, Annie's son hit them. It was a huge shock to the family. He did not know how he had died and only a few days later Mrs. Winter died as well. She died of a heart attack. It was a large funeral that saw them both buried together in the same plot in the East Finchley Cemetery. But the family rallied round and eventually got over their painful grief.

Some two years later, Terry was on a van delivery to a shop in Camden with driver Pete, when he mentioned he would drink at the Enterprise, a pub in Chalk Farm. He asked if Terry was free at the weekend and would he like to join him and his wife. Terry smiled and agreed to join them. He got the bus there and met Pete and his wife Ellen and their daughter, who was also called Ellen, who they had also brought along. They had a night to remember chatting incessantly and at the end of the evening Terry asked young Ellen on a date, and she accepted. He thought 'I've pulled!'.

When they started dating, Terry found it was a bit of a journey to Ellen's flat from his lodgings. She lived over a grocer's shop, with a fish factory at the back. It meant two buses to reach her. So, he bought an old bike. It wasn't great, but it was okay for his purposes of getting to Ellen's and for getting to work. But it was a struggle to cycle home after a late night in the pub with Ellen. Staying with Mary was now becoming awkward, so Charlie offered to have him stay at King's Cross.

However, by now, Terry and Ellen had decided to get married. Terry went to St. Aloysius church in Eversholt Street and booked the wedding date after declaring their bands. They rehearsed the marriage in the church and with this development, Charlie's housing offer was put on hold.

The day before the wedding, Terry still needed to get Ellen a wedding ring. He was told to go to the Chancery Lane jewelers on the recommendation of Charlie, where he managed to buy one for £6. Charlie also mentioned that the jockey, Ron Hutchison, had three rides that day as he knew Terry always liked to back him. So, Terry borrowed a couple of bob from Charlie, got to the bookies, put 2/- each way treble on the three horses and found

The Royal Ulster Rifles. Terry at the extreme right-hand side.

all three horses had won! Charlie could hardly believe it and came to the bookies to see Terry. They worked it out that he had won £100.16 shillings. He felt rich. So they went to the Sutton Arms where the reception was to be held, paid for the reception with £68, gave Ellen a few quid and of course paid back Charlie.

The Gods were smiling at Terry, and he felt a miracle had come his way, just at the right time as well.

8

The Wedding

Sheila and Boyd came down from Scotland to be at the wedding. And of course, all the Winters family were in attendance. The church was packed, and the service went according to plan. The best man was an army colleague from Dagenham. They had a fantastic party after the marriage and all the empty bottles were returned to the staff who paid Terry £13.

Ellen and Terry took over her parents' flat as the council had given them a flat in Hackney. So after the wedding, they went to the flat along with Bob his mate who slept on the settee and went home the next morning. As with all weddings, the day will be remembered well as many photos were taken. All seemed to wish to keep in touch and Terry was pleased that his sister and her husband got on well with the Winter family. More than ever, money was an important factor now he was married. Terry was still working at the wallpaper factory, so he was glad he had a bike rather than spend money on bus fares.

One of Terry's colleagues at the Wallpaper factory had a cousin called Lenny Brooks. He had a son, (also called Lenny) who was a plumber and worked around the Hampstead area for a man with a shop for yachting equipment. He doubled up as an agent for local clients for any plumbing jobs. Lenny asked if he'd like to learn plumbing and he immediately felt a change was needed as he was getting fed up with the wallpaper trade. Lenny was a cousin of the Winters, and his father was a car mechanic, so he was in good hands. He put in his notice and became a plumber's mate. It meant better pay and he would learn a useful trade. When he started, he had to go around big houses in Hampstead where many TV people lived, as well as famous names in politics and film. Over the years he got to meet Bill Oddie, John Freeman, Annie Lennox, Lynsey de Paul and Nicky Campbell as these were some of the celebrities' homes he repaired. The work was busy, and he'd get a few jobs done each day. Slowly, he learned how to fit new bathrooms. Hard work but he got the jobs done satisfactorily.

Ellen and Terry settled down to work and married life. Ellen had kept working at the job she had at a hairdresser's, the rent at their flat was cheap so they could buy regularly afford to buy the things they needed to furnish it.

One their first Christmas, Ellen's Mum and Dad came to visit and brought some lovely Christmas cards and birthday cards. Ellen's Dad had created them in old English calligraphy using coloured pens as it was his hobby. He also loved to create stone gnomes for the garden and Terry still has one that he gave them.

On Sundays, they would go to a pub in Pratt Street in Camden as it had winkles, cockles, prawns, and shrimps on the bar. If you were buying drinks, you could help yourself. Unusually, they even offered Scotch eggs.

It was also a live music pub and people would go up on stage, grab the microphone, and sing. On one occasion, Terry went up and sang two songs and by the applause, they seemed to like it. Soon he was singing regularly by request at the pub.

Ellen's grandfather was advanced in years. He lived in a big house on Regents Park Road with his wife. He used to work for a gin company called Gilbeys and one day he took Terry to see where all the old shire horses and the dray carts used for deliveries were housed in the stables at Camden Lock. It was a huge stable and there were many retired horses that had pulled the gin barrels in their time. The barrels were stored in a building called the Roundhouse, named because they stored barrels around the walls.

Nowadays it is no longer a stable. The stables are a market and the Roundhouse a concert hall, now popular with bands.

Terry continued to work hard and after a few years he passed his apprenticeship examinations, was able to do all plumbing work on his own and was now a plumber in his own right.

9

A Move to the East End

While reading the East London Advertiser one day, Terry saw a job seeking a maintenance man able to do plumbing repairs and general house jobs. The job came with free accommodation in a flat. He applied for the post and informed Lenny he would be packing in his job. He wished him good fortune and two weeks later they upped sticks and moved to Bethnal Green. The job was on an estate called the Winkley Estates and the flat was over the office. It contained two bedrooms, a lounge, no bathroom but a toilet on the landing with access to a balcony. There was a cooker and a sink on the landing as well. It was like a small kitchen where they could make their meals. The bedrooms were not bad for their size but the decoration was in poor condition, so there was much work to be done. The property also came with a garage. Inside was a full-sized console organ that belonged to the estate agent as he played in the church where he lived. He never heard him play it. He got to know all the tenants on the estate and would do the jobs he was given each day to keep the estate spick and span.

There were rows of cabinetmakers shops on the estate, and he had to do repairs for them as well, so there was much to keep him occupied. The estate also had a pub, the Flower Pot, a newspaper shop, greengrocers, butchers, a small chemist and a piano repair shop.

Ellen's brother, Tommy Gill, used to visit and he wondered if he could work with Terry. He worked in the city as a maintenance man for a hotel, so Tommy was taken on by the agent and began working with Terry. They worked with two buildings called Temple Dwellings and had fifty flats with old fireplaces and no bathrooms. When these residents wanted a bath, they went to the local council baths. They had a kitchen in each flat but just a sink and a concrete gas boiler for washing and a toilet. Tenants would buy coal and wood logs to use on the kitchen fire.

Next door was the grocers, owned by a Jewish couple with two sons. Terry could get groceries on tick in the week and pay when the wages came in. That's what was done in those days. As a Jewish family, they had their religious days when the sons would light the candles near the window. As the candles flickered, the boys would go to bed, upstairs. One night, their parents Morry and Fanny were in the shop and on the stairs were boxes of items which needed to be. The candles caught the net curtains in the window and smoke filled the house. Morry and Fanny tried to get to their sons, but because of the boxes hampering their progress upstairs, the parents could not get to one of their sons in time and he died of inhaling the smoke. The flat was severely burned and never returned to being a shop. The Jewish family continued to live on the estate though, so Terry could still get items on tick.

The Flower Pot pub was used by all the cabinetmakers and locals as it had a loan club which one joined and borrowed cash and paid back weekly. At the end of the year, one received a lump sum from the shares. It was a popular set-up, and many joined the club. By the door of the pub, a little old man called Harry Perry, an ex-boxer, had all his trophies around the bar. He was a sight to see. His son ran the pub. Harry sat by the fire warming the barley wine beers as they had to be warm, that was his job. Terry simply loved the pub's atmosphere. When Sheila and Boyd came to stay, they would go there and to the local markets along the high street in Bethnal Green and Roman Road. Shoreditch and the City were not too far away by bus or underground as well. They thoroughly enjoyed their visits to London.

Terry and Ellen went up to Scotland a couple of times and met many different people in a town called Kilmaurs. It's a small village where Sheila and Boyd had a flat on the main street in a place called The Murphy Buildings. Terry also met Boyd's mother and his brothers and sisters. His mother was aging and now lived in a prefabricated house just around the corner. She was well cared for by her family until her death. The rest of the family were close to Sheila and Terry considered them as being part of his extended family.

Back home in London, a short while later, Sheila announced she was going to get married. Ellen was chosen to be the Maid of Honour, so they traveled back north for the big occasion. It was a lovely day with all of Boyd's family, Sheila in her wedding dress and Ellen in her white suit and hat. It all turned out to be a wonderful day and Terry was so proud of his sister, Sheila.

After Sheila's wedding, they had not long arrived back in London when Ellen announced she was pregnant. Terry was over the moon. He looked forward to being a father. They set about finding a pram and other baby items. Eventually the big day came. Terry and Ellen had a son who they called Stephen.

Terry thought that they now needed a larger home and contacted the agent. He was told that it was only the flat that went with the job but as Terry got on well with the tenants and he didn't want to lose him, the agent secured them a bigger flat around the corner. So, once again they moved, this time into a flat over the workshops of the cabinetmakers.

To clear the property of numerous mice, a cat named Moggy took up residence with them. They had to sell the pram though, as it had two insurmountable staircases to negotiate. The answer was to buy a pushchair that folded and was easy to carry upstairs.

A wife, a child, a cat and now a car. Terry got hold of a Cortina, an early model, and booked himself a course of ten lessons. The last time he had driven a vehicle, he did so illegally, driving around the barracks in Ballymena! But he managed to pas his driving test the first time.

All this time he had still been thinking about and looking for any information on his mother. One day, Sheila suggested that as their mother had Irish origins, they should go to Ireland to search as there was always this bugging feeling that what Terry and Sheila knew wasn't the full answer. They decided that when his annual holiday came, he would go.

He decided he would make the trip using his car but that meant it would be the first time Terry had driven on a fast motorway. He didn't like it. He was exhausted. He was not going to go to Ireland alone, so Sheila went with him although as it turned out, the trip was mostly unsuccessful. After they returned from this trip, in a telegram from Sheila, he learned that she had given birth to a son, John.

Life in the East End was great. He got on well with most people on the estate and they all sent best wishes for the baby. The cabinetmakers made him welcome in the pub and they had a drink together. One of them said he knew Terry was good at his job as a plumber and he wondered if he had ever thought about going self-employed. Terry still had a year left on his contract with the agent, but it started a seed in his mind.

A short time after this, he went to King's Cross to visit young Mary who he had not seen for some time. While he was with her, Liz came in. Terry asked her if she knew anything about his mother. All she could say was that her mother had told her that

Terry's mother, Bridget, had lived on the Caledonian road and that she was buried at East Finchley. That took him no further forward but then she said Bridget had been flower seller in the Caledonian Road market.

Now this market, all these years ago, was the biggest market in the world. You could buy anything from pin cushions to coffins. She had worked with Tommy Barret, Mrs. Winter's brother, whom Terry had met at his wedding.

Terry looked up this market and it was true. It sold cattle which came by train to the market but there were hundreds of stalls with vegetables, meat, and all sorts of goods, too many to mention. Where 178 Caledonian Road was is today a row of shops but in days gone by, there were rooms in which people stayed and it was here that Bridget had had a room.

In the market, there was a story that a bull escaped its slaughter and ran down the road into the first open door and up the stairs on to the roof. When people tried to catch it, it jumped over the edge, crashed to the ground below and was killed instantly. Terry never knew if the story was a plausible tale. Sheila's son Neil (Terry's nephew) and Terry went to see the place but it was now open fields. However, the huge clock tower was still there. It's right opposite Pentonville Prison. Anyway, they enjoyed their day out together.

Another time, Terry and Ellen decided to go to Cornwall for a camping holiday with Ellen's best mate Brenda and her husband Dave. It was mentioned earlier that when Terry was in the army in Ballymena, he saw a man in the dining room who he thought he recognised and had promised to write to. Incredibly, Dave was that man! Terry couldn't believe it and they talked all about their time in the forces. He was a London taxi driver, owned his taxi and made a good living out of it. Dave was the funniest man he'd ever met and would have him in stitches. He would just run around in the morning singing "The hills are alive" and have the whole camp laughing. Everyone had a really good time. Both couples had their own tents and all the necessary camping equipment. Brenda was a real homely person and cooked some great food for them all. They had a son Dean who was turned out to be a good pal for Stephen. Terry just loved them all and kept his friendship with them for years. They have both sadly passed now, not long after each other and it was a massive upset for Terry, Ellen and Stephen at the time. But Terry still recalls them with fondness and the great memories he has of the time spent with them.

to like playing out in the garden hitting tennis balls but would often hit them over the fence into his neighbours greenhouse. They were always kind enough to return them but a cut-up tennis ball is of no use to anyone.

11

The Running Club

By this time, and after lots of training, Terry was getting much better at running. He entered a few of the race days in Victoria Park but often came in one of the trailers. Yet he could now run five miles without stopping. Not long after, he won a five-mile handicap race. The local press reported his victory with the banner headline "Brennan on the Boil!" Flushed with success, Terry decided to enter the London Marathon and finished in a noteworthy 4 hours 37 minutes.

Around this time, Ellen had found a new job as a house cleaner for TV's Christopher Biggins. As his home was near the running club, Terry would collect her if she left the house late, which she did on occasions. Because of this, Biggins gave Ellen a Morris Minor car which she learned to drive so she was able to get to herself to work and back.

As with most of the running clubs in those days, there was a bar and that's where the trophies were presented. Ellen often came to these award presentations, but Biggins also used to take her to TV shows with him where she met other celebrities. One of the many perks that went with her job.

Ellen took Terry along to a couple of the shows that Biggins was in, where he also got to meet and shake the hands of famous faces of the day such as Cilla Black, the singer Johnny Mathis and the actress Marti Webb but it wasn't for him. The few times he went was enough of the celebrity life for Terry.

Terry preferred being at the running club and shortly after was appointed president. Presenting prizes to winners as president was a pleasant duty but there were a couple of runners who used to goad him about it when they were in the showers and around the club. It made him feel so uncomfortable, so he resigned from the presidency. He completed another London Marathon, but returned in a slower time than his first. Back at the club, he struck up a friendship with an Irishman who was also a runner at the club, Jimmy Edmond, and they ran everywhere. They thought nothing of running from Victoria Park to Camden Lock and back to the club for a pint or two. Another one of the clubs' runners, Albert Balbi joined them on a marathon, and he caused a stir. They were approaching the finishing line when Balbi stopped. He asked a woman who was watching, as he noticed she was smoking, for a fag. Albert lit it up and finished the race smoking. The loudspeaker announced, "...and here comes Balbi with a fag in his mouth!" Everyone collapsed with laughter. It was so funny. Terry had some very happy days at the club, and it made him a lot fitter.

12

A Holiday in Sweden

By this time, Stephen was old enough to start working. He had managed to get a job on the Underground at Baker Street for London Transport. He enjoyed the work and left home each day with a spring in his step. He was transforming from a boy into a man.

One night at a social club in Leyton they often used to visit, they met a Swedish couple, Bengt and Sue, and got on so well with them that they invited them back for dinner. It was not a complete surprise then for an invitation to Sweden to come their way the following summer.

After flying to Stockholm, they met Bengt as he had an office there and he showed them around the city. It struck Terry how clean the city was. There was a huge man-made lake in centre and after the tour, Bengt drove them to his house in the country, which was a fair distance from Stockholm. During their stay they went fishing on one of the many lakes, catching large trout which they ate on the country's Feast Day, which celebrates Birgitta, the patron saint of Sweden. Bengt gave them Aktavit, a distilled spirit that is made in Scandinavia as it accompanied the raw fish with almonds but of course, due to its potency

(100% proof!), they decided to have just small shot of the alcohol. All in all, Terry thought it was a marvelous holiday, and noticed that Stephen and Ellen loved the place as well and seemed at home. Terry had hopes that Stephen, being of an age now, might like their daughter, possibly bringing some Viking blood into the family, but it was not to be. They kept in touch for some time afterward, but it was one of those friendships that just peter out naturally.

13

The Church in Leyton

Stephen was now well established at work, and he started to learn to read music, playing an organ at lessons once a week, gradually learning 48 songs over time. Stephen got the hang of it quickly, but Terry, who was also learning to play was much slower. He'd previously bought an organ and practiced on it a lot so if anyone from Stephen's class asked, he thought he could play at the next lesson. Terry could only read music a bit and although not yet fluent, he was well on the way.

On a Sunday they would all go to the local church, St. Josephs in Francis Road where they hoped, perhaps one day, Stephen might marry. In fact, he had previously spotted a girl he liked sitting with her parents up front in the church. He built up the courage to ask her out, to which she said yes. Soon, they came to visit each of their parental homes, and both sets of parents suspected a serious relationship was underway. A short while later they decided to get married. The priest from the church made all the arrangements and shortly after, Stephen was married to Julie. Terrys can recall all of this with great detail but for the life of him, he can't remember where they had their honeymoon!

They eventually bought a flat in the same road as the church and settled in. Terry and Ellen had always been proud parents of Stephen, and now felt proud parents of the couple. They continued to go to the church as they thought it would be handy for christenings!

As Terry felt Ellen was very settled in her work and her daily life, he asked her if she wouldn't mind if he went to Scotland and take the opportunity to walk the West Highland Way with Sheila. Ellen said yes so he went up to stay with Sheila and they set out on the 95-mile trek from Milngavie to Fort William.

Later that year, Terry and Ellen took Stephen and Julie with them to Greece and had a great time was had by all. Shortly after returning, Ellen decided she wanted to become a Roman Catholic. That meant instruction from the priest, which she took and in due course, Ellen became a Catholic. Terry thought that would augur well when Stephen and Juie had their first child, Daniel, and later a second boy, Jamie, christened in the

Stephen Brennan

church. Terry and Ellen were thrilled with the grandchildren that had come their way and were pleased that they got to see them frequently.

Stephen and Julie had Terry fit a bathroom suite, replace the floorboards in the lounge, replace joists, and even fit a new boiler in their home as they were looking to sell their flat now that they had two children. That must have helped as soon after they put up the asking price, sold the flat and moved to a new house.

14

Suspicion

Terry was still running and would still pick up Ellen sometimes from work. Occasionally though, when he came home straight from work there would be a guy from the running club in the house. One time, it was his running mate Albert and on another occasion, someone else. Terry was getting suspicious about this, and it began to cause arguments. One day when he went to pick up Ellen from Biggins, she was in the house opposite, which on occasion she would. This house was owned by someone called John and his wife Pam. John had a dovetailing business on the estate he had worked on and Terry knew him well, so it was no surprise to find her there as she would often pop in to see them after finishing work with Biggins. His wife Pam was a lovely person, but she had a long-term illness. As a group, they used to go to a restaurant on the canal with Biggins and his friends, as Pam and John knew Biggins as well.

One night not long after this, Terry was at home when the phone rang. It was Pam. She was screaming and shouting at Terry telling him to keep Ellen away from her husband, accusing Ellen of having an affair with her husband. Shortly after this happened, Pam died. Her long-term illness was more serious than anyone realised and the very next day, Ellen told Terry that she was leaving him for John and wanted a divorce, after 29 years of marriage.

Terry was shocked to the core. He returned to the club and ran. But he was in a mess. He could not believe what Ellen had just told him. The boys at the club were naturally shocked too and consoled him as much as they could, as did Sheila when he phoned her. She was as upset about it as he was.

Life goes on though, so Terry went back to work and had a very busy day. He was exhausted when he returned home. But when he opened the door, he saw things were different somehow. He went to the bedroom and noticed the empty wardrobe. Ellen and packed up and left. The solicitor's letter came next. It gave notice of a divorce hearing in Stratford Magistrate's court. While he awaited that court appointment, he threw himself into work, went to the pub as usual as he liked to sing, and met many more like-minded souls. He called at a pub in Bethnal Green for one drink and met a woman called Barbara. They chatted, got on well and agreed to go on a date.

The day of the Magistrate's court dawned. He went in his suit, but was feeling sick. The experience was horrible. The Judge acknowledged Terry was the man source of income, had paid all the bills and also contributed to the household. The ruling was that Terry would make a settlement of a one-off payment to Ellen but could keep the house and its contents. The divorce was then finalised.

He left the court feeling he that he had never felt so bad in all his life, especially after 29 years of marriage, but Barbara was there, as Terry had started to see her quite frequently, and she helped to comfort him.

To put those terrible days behind him, Terry headed north to be with Sheila. To help him get a fresh start, they decided to walk the West Highland way again. The walk took six days. This is a tough walk across some beautiful countryside and up some very rough roads leading to Glen Coe and the Devil's Staircase to the top of the mountain and onto Loch Rannoch. They slept in a bivouac tent. One morning as Terry peered out of the tent, he was looking at a huge pair of antlers, a deer just stood there. Their eyes fixed on each other and they stared at each other for what seemed like ages to Terry. Terry was just waiting for him to charge in the tent when he turned and headed towards the hotel a short distance away. Apparently, everyone in the hotel knew of this deer as he used to raid the dustbins for food!

When they arrived at Fort William, he was shattered but in retrospect, this was just what he needed to get over Ellen's fateful decision and turn a new page in his life. He stayed with Sheila for two more days before he returned to Leyton. The house felt very lonely when he returned but Stephen and Julie came round with their sons. He cooked dinner for them, and slowly but surely, he recovered to sense of normality, in the company of Barbara, who he was now seeing regularly.

15

Barbara, my new partner

Terry's work was getting busier. Biggins had recommended him to new private customers that wanted plumbing work done. One was TV personality and actress Linda Bellingham, who amongst other things, was well known for the OXO adverts she did over the years. Terry thought she was the nicest of people and ended up doing a lot of work for her.

One day Linda told Terry that she'd love to visit an east-end pub and meet real people, as it were, but felt strange about just turning up at one at random.

So, one Saturday night, Terry took her to an east-end pub called the Queen Victoria, just off from Columbia Road, where a famous Sunday flower market is held. She had a great time mixing with the many people that were there. They didn't make a fuss of her and treated her just like everyone else, although they all knew she was a well-known actress. Linda told Terry later that she had loved that response and had really enjoyed the pub's atmosphere.

Another one of his famous customers was Barbara Kelly, who was best known for her television roles in the UK opposite her husband, Bernard Braden in the 1950s and 1960s, and for her many appearances on the TV quiz show "What's my Line?"

She had a house in Alexandra Park which she once lived in but it was now empty. The builders were renovating it and Terry had to put a water tank in the loft space. As he cleared away a space for the water tank, he came across photos of Barbara and her husband, Bernard. So, he kept hold of them with the intention of returning them to her. When he managed to obtain her agent's address, he sent the photos back to her. Barbara wrote to Terry to thank him for the photos which meant a lot to her.

At the end of the letter, she informed him that she was writing a book and would mention Terry in her book. She enclosed photographs of herself and her husband which he still has.

Barbara (Terry's new friend) and he met regularly, and she would come round to help clean his house while she still had a flat in Bethnal Green. After a while socializing in pubs and on walks, Barbara moved in with Terry and she put her flat out to rent. Terry had sold his boat some time ago and purchased a caravan in Dovercourt in Essex, so they went away for weekends

To Terry with a Thousand Thanks Barbara Kelly

in it and relaxed. Terry felt his new life couldn't get much better, part of which was his blossoming relationship with Barbara, so much so that they decided to let her family and friends make use of the caravan when they were not using it.

Sheila came down to stay with them and they set off on walks in Constable country at Flatford Mills and walks not too far from the sea at Harwich. We nicknamed the pub called the Trafalgar in Harwich the fish shop, as they used to put prawns and other shellfish on the bar on a Sunday. Terry purchased an old rickety bike there and used to use it go do the shopping for

Barbara and Terry also went to Margate for a weekend to stay at Butlin's Holiday Park. Butlin's provided a lot of various entertainment in the main building, one of which was Karaoke nights which often featured a guy called Karaoke Joe. He was an elderly man and he always sang the same song every time and we all loved him for it. While there, they enjoyed a walk to Broadstairs and back along the coast road. Barbara could walk well then even though it was a long way but nowadays, due to her age and health problems, it would be difficult. All in all, they had some great weekends away.

When they arrived back in London, they visited Barbara's sister June, who lives in Gospel Oak. June was in the kitchen and asked how they enjoyed the weekend. Barbara said to her that Terry took her on a long walk to Broadstairs and back and June replied, 'how far is that?' Barbara told her that Terry reckoned it was about twelve miles. June said. 'Oh, you poor little sod. Couldn't you have found someone with a car?'

We all burst out laughing. June was a lovely person, and I thought a lot of her. She was so gentle.

At this time, she wasn't too well and her daughter Mandy was caring for her.

Ahead of the move to Scotland, Terry had asked his sister if she knew of anyone with a caravan as they had decided that they would live in one temporarily until they could find a house. He had already sold his caravan at Dovercourt a while before. Along with this, they arranged for all their possessions to be taken to Kilmarnock in Ayrshire, as Sheila knew of a storage depot there. Sheila replied saying that she knew of one going for £4,000, so Terry immediately forwarded a bank draft to her before they left which meant they would have a caravan waiting for them when they arrived. When the furniture lorry arrived at Terry's house in Leyton, he was surprised that such a large vehicle could negotiate the cul-de-sac let alone carry all their items, but it did.

When they arrived at the site, which was on a hill by the sea in a town called Auchenlarie, they found that it was ideal for them to live in it until they found a house. Terry found a buyer for his van and bought a jeep, but it wasn't one of his best purchasers. The jeep struggled on hills, but it would do for the present.

16

Lucy

The caravan was 37 feet long and had two bedrooms, a diner, a shower room, a good-sized kitchen and a balcony with railings where they could sit outside and have meals while watching the sea down the hill to a small bay. On the caravan site was a clubhouse with a large sitting area, a bar, a swimming pool and a games room with a pool table. Sheila and Boyd would come down to visit them and in the caravan next to theirs was a couple of people from Sheila and Boyd's town. They got to know them quite well and that helped seal another friendship. There was even Saturday night Karaoke and sometimes a live band to dance to.

Barbara expressed a wish to have a dog and Terry had no objection as Sheila had a collie called Megan who he was quite fond of. Boyd said there was a police dog pound in a nearby village to his home looking to rehome dogs. Terry went up and Boyd took them to the compound. All the dogs, of different ages, were in metal cages. As they progressed down the line, one dog licked Terry's hand as he passed by and he stopped. He went no further. And so, after paying a fee of £20, Terry was allowed to take this dog. He bundled her into the car and spoke to her as he drove back to the caravan.

As soon as Barbara saw the dog, she cuddled it and the dog responded by making a fuss of her too. The decided to call her Lucy. They took her to the vet who told them that the dog was only a puppy, about 5 months old. She was given an injection and a clean bill of health.

The boys in the next caravan were playing outside as they often did, but Lucy was skittish. Terry sat with her to watch the boys and slowly the she took to them. But when Sheila brought Megan down with her to visit, Lucy immediately took to Megan and the dogs would play together. They had brought a fluffy duck toy and the two dogs would grab hold of it and play tug-of-war. The duck became very frayed, so it was sewn up again and again. Terry can't remember how many times it had to be sewn up, but Barbara will, as she was usually the one doing the sewing! In time, Lucy adapted really well and was soon able to be off the

Lucy and Briah

lead and respond to the call. Terry placed netting around the caravan base so Lucy could be outside without wandering off, but she just nosed her way under the netting, lifting out the pegs. To counteract this, they decided to get stronger pegs from B&Q, but no sooner had they left the store when the alarm sounded. Apparently, the pegs had little tags on, which they thought were included in the price! But the girl at the till understood. The summoning of Her Majesty's Constabulary was not required on this occasion and all was well afterwards.

Life in the caravan was quite good but of course, a house was still required. They had looked for houses in Prestwick, Ayr, and Girvan but they were all too pricey. One bungalow in a village called New Abbey was much cheaper and they did put an offer in, but the agent informed them that the house was already off the market. He also said they didn't want any English in the village. Terry was going to take this situation further but decided not to as the village was too far from shops anyway and they just forgot about that. It did niggle them though. It just wasn't very nice of them. Not long after this, while looking through the local estate's weekly paper, Terry saw one in Dumfries about eighteen miles from the caravan site that looked promising. They drove there and found it was a newly built house just six years old. It cost £48,000 so they bought it and paid in cash.

It had two bedrooms, a large lounge, a fitted kitchen, a bathroom upstairs, a reasonably sized garden with a shed at the back and the front was big enough for three cars. But the décor was atrocious and the colour scheme had to be changed.

Once they were settled in their new house, Terry changed the Jeep for a Vauxhall hatchback, which was especially useful for the dog. He got it from a friend of Sheila's called Bobby Bain who repaired and sold cars. Sheila knew him as he lived in the same village. Bobby also managed to sell the jeep for him.

On the outskirts of Dumfries is a place called Maybie Forest.

It has at least four different walks, between eight and twelve-miles. It's a lovely place and Lucy loved it and Terry would take her there quite often. There is a large hotel there, the Maybie Forest, which you can dine at. They ate there once, but Terry and Barbara considered it a bit expensive. He could always take Lucy to Sheila and Boyd's home anytime if they were going away as everyone loved Lucy. She was a really loveable character.

That summer Terry was busy in the house and garden. He had decorated it throughout with Gardenia, and everyone agreed it looked beautiful. He formed a border around the edges for plants and ordered a conservatory kit from a company in Cornwall. It came on a huge lorry and Terry had already got planning permission to for it as it required a concrete base, block walls to the neighbours side and a low wall with patio doors. After construction it received its official pass from the planning inspectors, and they used to sit out in it in the summer. It was so relaxing.

Terry and Barabara decided take a break, and with Lucy left at Sheila's, went down to London travelling by train from Carlisle. They stayed at Barbara's niece Mandy's in Gospel Oak as by this time, June had sadly passed and the house now belonged to Mandy. As Terry had already said, they always got on well, so they dined out with Mandy a few times and of course visited the local pub.

While down in London, Terry went to the Finchley cemetery to tend to his mother's grave. The weeds had grown again, and he spent some time removing them. It was not an easy task but his love for his mother urged him on. Terry also went to Caledonian Road to see if he could find any of the Winter family, but it seemed they had all had moved away. Terry realised a long time had passed since he saw any of them and perhaps now some of them may even be dead. Number 10 Southern Steet had long been demolished with new flats erected in its place.

Terry hardly recognised it, nor Calshot Street which had had a similar clearance. It was sad to see so many places he had loved disappear, but as with all things, change is inevitable

On their return to Dumfries, Sheila and Terry agreed that they should try to find out something more about their parents so they made a date to go to Ireland. Barbara decided to stay with Lucy in Dumfries and Boyd supported the quest to find out more about his in-laws

17

Ireland

Terry booked a caravan in Bennetsbridge, near Kilkenny for a week and after picking up Sheila, they drove down to the Liverpool docks for the eight-hour crossing. All the time they were on it, they had to stay in the upstairs lounge of this ferry, full of containers and cars, until they docked in Dublin, but this is the case with most ferries. It was quite an experience on the ferry as there were many big muscled men, mostly lorry drivers, who continually filled their plates at the all-inclusive restaurant/cafe, but the passengers did too. You could choose whatever you wished from the self-service and go for extras at no additional cost. Everyone seemed so very friendly, although obviously none knew what their business would be in Ireland. Terry and Sheila did not reveal it either, as they would have had the most unusual mission to explain.

After they docked in the capital, Sheila got down to map-reading. She was good at that and soon they were at the campsite. After settling in, they set off on their quest so drove into Kilkenny, a gaily painted town with colourful shops and cafes and in the center of the town, stood a huge Church for all to see. They had no difficulty getting parked, but before starting out they sat down and had lunch and felt very much abroad in this beautiful Irish town.

They were directed to Rothe House on the main street where all the records were kept so walked to the register office. After explaining to an official at the office the nature of their enquiry, he told them he would look for records while a woman started to find certificates. She found a Bridget Brennan neé O'Brien, whose mother's name was Mary English. She had lived in Kilkenny and was born in the workhouse there. It may not be the right Bridet Brennan they were told, although that thought had already passed his mind. However, they were then directed to the workhouse in town.

As it was a distance from the register office they drove there and found it to be a big old grey stonework building. It looked locked up, at first sight, but on the side of the building was a door. They knocked and a man opened it. He asked if he could help them. Terry showed his collection of papers which he had cherished and maintained. He confirmed that Bridget Brennan neé O'Brien was born there and her mother, Mary English. Although they were now convinced they had found where she spent her early years, the man told them that a lot of children born there were paupers and in those days, especially in a deeply religious country such as Ireland, to get pregnant was a sin if not married. He showed them where the babies were bathed and showed them a lot of rooms where they slept. It was an eerie place, and you could feel how desperate those people must have been. They were shown the patch where vegetables were cultivated, but it was now derelict and overgrown. One could literally smell how old the place was from the dusty rooms and out sheds. It's now a heritage site. Many mothers and children did not survive the harsh conditions of this life. A cart would call each day to collect bodies and, if you managed to survive, you were eventually put out on the streets to fend for yourself. The place was eerie and even spooky. He said he would take them along the road to Berryfield to show them where all the babies were buried.

It was a field, fenced in with just grass growing but he told them they were standing on around 3,000 bodies in the ground. There was just one large stone in the middle of the field. That was for the last Nun who was buried there. There was a plaque there to tell what the field was and all that had happened there before. It was the saddest sight they had ever seen. At times, it would have been even sadder as after heavy rain, the bodies would surface and had to be re-buried. Sheila and Terry would never forget that place.

As Mrs. Winters had said that their mother Bridget was married to a Patrick Thomas Brennan in St Peter's church in Kilkenny, they had asked at Rothe House where this church was. Apparently, it wasn't too far to walk there. But the small church they had been directed to was a Protestant church in Thomastown and they immediately knew that it wasn't the right one. They were confused. So they returned to Rothe House and were then directed to a vicarage at a place called Nenagh which wasn't far by car. They hoped that the priest there would be able to shed some light so that spurred them onwards.

At the vicarage, the priest apologised and told them he was in a rush to attend a wedding reception. The priest got in his car and took off like a rocket. They followed him at what seemed like break-neck speeds when suddenly, the priest put his hand out of the window and directed them along another road. We found the building that looked like an office that would keep records and went in. A man appeared and after they told them of their mission, he ran off a list of all the family but started to laugh. They wondered what was so funny, so he told them they were sitting in a prison cell and gave them a card to prove it. Terry and Sheila laughed as well, feeling he probably told all his visitors this strange story.

He gave them lots of copies of various certificates and when they got back to the caravan, they went through them and felt what they had was true. It had been a long tiring day, so they ordered a taxi and went to a local pub. The people inside could tell they were strangers, but they were made to feel welcome. They were asked to sit in front of the bar for a photo. Little did they know that the barman behind them was making faces when the photos were taken!

Then the music began. A couple took center stage to sing and play guitar then a man played the Bodhran, a traditional Irish drum. Music suddenly filled the bar. They gave a wonderful performance and Terry and Sheila enjoyed their relaxed evening in the pub's company. They got back in the taxi late that evening and got ready to travel the next morning. They were returning to Dumfries.

The return trip was uneventful, and the next day Terry phoned his son to inform him of what little he had found out in Ireland.

18

Dean and Jackie's wedding

Barbara's son Dean and his fiancé Jackie were getting married, and Barbara and Terry went to Barking in East London for the occasion. Barbara had crocheted a dress and her hat and handbag in blue. It was amazing. Terry had never seen anything like it before. No wonder it had taken her some time to make. It would almost steal the show. It looked so good.

The wedding in the register office was a grand occasion and afterward, they all went to a pub for the reception where each person could choose any meal from the pubs menu rather than have a set meal. It was a good idea. Lots of photos were taken and we all had a great chinwag which made it a great evening with the couple, their friends, and the two families.

The couple had bought a house in Dagenham, and we returned to visit it. Barbara was impressed by it, as was Terry. When they returned home, Barbara told all and sundry about the wedding. Dean is a computer graphic designer and does most of his work with large corporate companies and his wife Jackie is a British Sign Language interpreter and works in care homes and hospitals as required. But they did not stay long in Dagenham. They moved to Hastings on the south coast with their beautiful golden retrievers, Sadie and Leela. Terry and Barbara would enjoy going down to visit them, one of the highlights being going in to Hastings Old Town, where they stood in line for a fish roll from a shack on the seafront called Pat & Tush's. It was basically a bread roll with two flounders, fried in a tray of oil. Despite it's simpleness they were delicious. It was thoroughly enjoyable to walk along the seafront while eating them and it was an enjoyable visit. The train line down to Hastings goes through Orpington station where Terry went to school and that brough back some memories. Whenever Barbara and Terry go down to London, they get on the train and go down to stay with them.

Many years after they first visited them in Hastings, Dean and Jackie had rescued a new golden retriever called Ziggy, as by this time, Sadie and Leela had passed. Dean would walk Ziggy in their local woods and on one occasion, Terry joined him. The place is called Church-in-the-Woods as deep into the woods, unsurprisingly, is a church. It was called St Leonard's Church, an Anglican church. So, Terry asked Dean to wait while he went in where he was welcomed by a man who was with a group of locals. Terry asked if he could have a look around. A lady took him around the church and explained the origins of the windows and the many statues and the main altar and much more.

He was a stranger to them, but they made him feel so welcome. He took photos of the church which is very old with lots of history, and later read up about it on Google. Ziggy just thinks he owns the woods as he knows every other dog and his way all around the grounds. He is a very charming boy. The wood is in a place called Hollington, an area of the town of St Leonard's. Terry recommends anyone who visits the woods to take the time to go and see this picturesque church.

19

John's Wedding

Sheila's son John, left London to work for his building company as a senior quantity surveyor in Nassau in the Bahamas. He had met a schoolteacher, Andrea, who was Canadian. Terry flew up to Canada to meet her parents a few times. The family received their invitations to the wedding on the island. Terry had bought a suit from a tailor in Bethnal Green before they left London. It was the same shop where the Kray twins used to buy their suits! Shiela had arranged for her sons to be kilted.

It was a ten-hour flight to the island and Terry and Barbara were booked into a hotel called The Breezes. It was huge and seemed mainly to cater to the American market as the USA is nearby. The Americans do like the best and the hotel was just that. Terry loved their crab salad. There were three swimming pools, with colourful hummingbirds flying around the bushes. They showed no fear and would perch within arm's length. The wedding was set on a jetty out at sea under a shady canopy of local flowers. Sheila's boys looked splendid in their kilts and Andrea looked spectacular in her wedding dress. Sheila and Barbara looked photogenic and Boyd, being the proud father, played his part well.

Thankfully, as it mostly does in the Bahamas, the sun shone lighting up the whole scene. After the service, they retreated to the restaurant on the beach for the meal, more photos and speeches. Then on to the Matison hotel, next to theirs, where they had drinks, and met a lot of John and Andrea's family, John's workmates and many guests. It was a wonderful wedding. They stayed in the Bahamas for another three weeks. One day they were all taken by a big boat to an island for a barbeque and took along food and beer to a sandy bay overlooking a house a short distance away. It was Sean Connery's home. It was colossal. They watched the sun dip on their way back to the beach and suddenly the sunset disappeared. A couple of times Terry went with John to the cricket club, but those days are over now, John eventually moved off the island and settled in Atlanta, Georgia. They bought a huge house in a private development, about forty miles outside Atlanta.

20

Back in Dumfries

There was still a job of work to do at the house in Dumfries. Terry hired a builder to build a garage at the side of the house but he made all the trusses for the roof and tiled it himself. An electric garage door was also installed. He had the front block paved with two diamond shapes. It looked good. A problem also existed on his property because local kids were climbing over his side fence, so Terry nailed carpet gripper all along the top of the fence and the problem ended. Luckily, no one got hurt. After all this work was done, they took a break to go up to Sheila as her son Neil had booked a lodge up in Perthshire at Rannoch Moor. But it snowed that night, nearly four inches deep but as they had their dogs with them, they loved it. Terry struggled to get the car along the road back to the airport at ten miles an hour for nine miles for Neil and his partner Mario's flight back to London, but eventually they made it.

Back home Tony, Terry's next-door neighbour, introduced Terry to fly fishing. He took lessons from a Gillie (an ancient Celtic term for a person who acts as an attendant on a fishing or hunting expedition) near Annan and after ten lessons he was able to fly fish.

He caught lots of trout but found them rather bland to eat, so gave most of what he caught to various friends. But Terry found that he enjoyed the sport so he ended up belonged to the fishing club for thirteen years.

Soon after this break, they received a message that Neil and Mario were to get married. Mario is Brazilian and is well-suited to Neil. So once more it was off to London, staying at Mandy's. Sheila and Boyd stayed with Neil in London at a house he was renovating.

21

Neil's wedding

Neil and Marios wedding was a civil one and was arranged to be at Chelsea Town Hall. On the day of the wedding, Terry met up with Sheila and Boyd and made their way to Chelsea. At the Town Hall, lots of Mario's family were there and they all got to meet them and his friends. The wedding ceremony went well and when it ended, they all walked to the river Thames where at the pier, they boarded a cruise boat, which was to be the venue for the reception. Lots of food and drink was available and dancing obviously took place as the boat went travelled along to Windsor and then returned to Tower Bridge. Mario could do the salsa particularly well and danced with his sister. Neil had been telling people about Terry and Sheila's search for their parents. Terry said he was thinking about a gravestone. Neil said he would attend to that, and he ordered a beautiful blue headstone with their mother's name on it. Terry thought that the whole day was wonderful.

When the headstone was ready, Terry contacted John and they all went to lay it. It was a lovely day as all of Mario's family stood around while John and Neil laid it. It looked beautiful and both Terry and Sheila were so pleased with it that Terry

Bridget's headstone

said he wanted to be buried in the same spot when his time came.

Meanwhile, Terry repeated his vow to keep the grave clear of debris and unnecessary growth to keep it clean, and when that was done, he would lay flowers on her grave.

Running five London marathons and several half-marathons had taken its toll on Terry's knees, so much so that he had to have a replacement operation on his left one. The operation was performed at Dumfries and Galloway Royal Infirmary, and Terry had to follow up his operation with physiotherapy at the same place. So in the end, all the running did his legs little good. When he sees people running on the roads, he wants to tell them to run on grass as the road running will eventually take its toll. However, despite this he continued to enjoy walking. He once again finished the West Highland Way. Shelia and Terry walked it three times together over the years and Sheila herself, four times. At times he wished he had taken up walking instead of running. It's so much more enjoyable.

His nephew John decided that he wanted to do the London marathon and he did it in a good time. As he passed Terry and Sheila, she said to Terry that lots of people were running for Flora. He told her everyone was as Flora was the sponsor of the race. They both laughed, it was so funny.

22

Return to Ireland

The next time Terry was at Sheila's, they decided to go back to Ireland with what they had learned and pick up where they had left off. Terry had a letter from a Mrs. Sharkey in Dublin saying that she had found information on what Rothe House had given them the last time they were over, so they fixed a time to return. Sheila and Boyd came down to stay with him and the next day both Sheila and Terry headed to Stranraer to catch the ferry to Belfast. They would drive from there down to Fiddown near Waterford, where they rented the old Post Office, which was now a holiday cottage. Neil and Mario flew over to the nearby airport at Waterford and Terry went to meet them, taking them with him to the post office to stay. The rooms were quaint and the original shelves with Marmite jars and old antiques on them were lovely. Then it was down to work at hand with many heads to help.

They had certificates of a Bridget O'Brien and her parents Mary O'Brien and Patrick Thomas O'Brien. They also felt that Bridget was born in the workhouse in Kilkenny. Rothe House had given them a birth certificate of Bridget showing 1902. Bridget was born in Callan workhouse. John O'Brien was the father and

Mary O'Brien was the mother whose maiden name was English. They had five children: namely Bridget, Kate, Patrick, John, and William. The family moved around a lot and the census of 1911 showed different areas as Thomas was a laborer. So, they decided to travel to Graiguemanagh and visit the local priest in nearby Duiske Abbey in the town. They sat with him and looked at his records. Yes, indeed a Bridget was baptized there.

Mary and John O'Brien were not on record as having married in the town but a record in a chapel in Wexford Registrar's records shows that they were married there in 1900. They were now convinced they were on the right track. They returned to Kilkenny and agreed that what Mrs. Winter had said about a St Peter's church in Kilkenny was not true. Still, not completely sure if they had got things right, all five of them went to the pub that night and spent the evening in boisterous company with the locals. They had really fallen in love with the town.

When they were all back home, Terry contacted Mrs. Sharkey in Dublin and told her they had been over to Kilkenny and what they had found. He asked if she had an address of any living person who knew the O'Brien family in Waterford as he thought it might be good idea to write to them. He also asked if she knew of a Kate O'Brien as they had a certificate of her birth.

He felt it might give them a connection. Sheila wrote to another official and got a reply saying there was no certificate of a Kate O'Brien that she knew, so it seemed like yet another dead end. Mrs. Sharkey was still conducting a search on their behalf, but it was becoming very complicated now as O'Brien was a common name and to pin down the right one was proving difficult. So, they decided to leave the quest for the time being but kept in touch with a genealogist they had made contact with in Dublin. However, she eventually reached a point where said she could do no more and thanked Terry for his enquiries. He sent her a final payment although she was kind enough to continue to send a lot more certificates and suggestions as to what he could do next. Rothe House had recommended that Terry write to a man named Danny Grace in a town called Nenagh as his family had knowledge of the O'Brien family. He received a reply that his uncle knew of the O'Brien family, and where they went to school, but the O'Brien's that he knew of were a different family so there was no joy there either, but he was grateful that he had replied, nevertheless. Sheila had meanwhile written to someone else who knew of a family of O'Brien's that lived in Co. Carlow, but that led nowhere either.

They were still not sure about where they were in the work, but Terry and Sheila both thought they would keep trying to see if they could get any more leads from their contacts.

Back home in Kilmaurs, Sheila had found some work for a Norwegian couple called Per and Anne Halverson, who lived in her village. They had a lovely home, just a short distance from Sheila and Boyd's house. Sheila cleans for Anne and does additional housework. Anne is Scottish and Per, the Norwegian, was very interested in Genealogy. One day Sheila was chatting to them about the genealogy search she and her brother were engaged in. He was interested in looking at all their past paperwork. Terry and Sheila did not immediately realise it, but this was a seminal moment in their search.

23

A Heart Attack

Terry got up one morning and he couldn't breathe. He struggled on the floor to call Barbara and she came racing into the bedroom. She took one look at him and dialed for an ambulance. When the medics arrived, he struggled to tell them what was wrong, as he found it hard to speak to them. Within five minutes he was in the ambulance, attached to various tubes and a sizeable machine he had never seen before, and was immediately taken to hospital. Suddenly doctors were around him, telling him he had had a heart attack. It was a severe angina and the specialist informed Terry that a triple bypass was required which meant surgery at Glasgow.

The Jubilee Hospital, which was once a hotel, had been donated to Glasgow. It still has the hotel attached to the main building. This is where all the heart surgery is performed. Families are allowed stay there for the duration of their loved ones surgery. It had a large dining area with different foods, which were very enjoyable. When Terry's operation was due, he was just about to go under the knife when a doctor appeared and told him his operation would have to be delayed as a pregnant woman with a heart disease was about to go for surgery. They told him her case was a priority, but he pleaded with them as they had already given him a sedative in preparation for the operation. He was told that his operation would be the same day, so he was quite relieved.

After the operation, he was taken to the intensive care room and was placed in a chair on his own. That was when he began to hallucinate. He thought the cupboards were on fire. He called the nurse and told her about the fire, but she calmed Terry down and then transferred him to a ward with other people.

Stephen flew up from London to be with him. Sheila and Boyd came each day and Barbara was at hand as well as Boyd's longtime friend, Jock Forsythe, who also came to visit so he was certainly not alone. After five days he was released to travel home. The NHS provided him with a taxi paid for by them. But before he left the hospital, Terry asked the nurses how he could repay them. They told him that nurses have to pay for their coffee and tea themselves. So, when the taxi arrived in Dumfries the driver was asked to wait while Barbara went to a shop and returned with several boxes of coffee and tea and the driver was asked to deliver the goods to the nurses in the ward. They phoned with their thanks the following day. Terry remained very sore for a few weeks as his chest had plasters all over it and his legs had a similar amount too. As you would expect, he was out of action for quite a while.

24

Mandy's Wedding in London

After a period of recuperation, Terry was starting to feel much better. A good few weeks had passed when Barbara received a message that Mandy was getting married, and she had asked that Terry give her away, as her father had passed many years before. He was naturally honored and chuffed to have been asked. So out came all the best clothes again and they got ready to go south by train.

They arrived at Mandy's and spent a few days with her before her big day arrived. On that special day, they all had to report to Camden Town Hall where an old red London Bus had been hired and as soon as they got on, the music started. Champagne was under the seats and the bus took them to Camden, singing as they went, with pedestrians and passersby cheering them on their way. Probably due to nerves, Terry needed to dash to the wee small room as soon as they arrived. The it was time to accompany Mandy as the ceremony started. He was so proud to be walking down the aisle with her. She had a lot of bridesmaids that all wore the same dresses and they were stunning. Mandy had the most beautiful red dress and she was a real picture.

After the ceremony, everyone was taken on the bus to

Blackfriars's Bridge to a pub called Doggett's as Mandy and her new husband Charlie, had booked the top floor for the reception. The drinks were flowing, and the food was most appetizing. Eventually, they got late taxis home. What a day was had.

While they were down in London, Terry arranged to meet his son Stephen at Camden Lock. There, Terry told him about Sheila's new Norwegian friend who was a keen family researcher. Per had suggested to Terry to request a DNA sample which they decided to do. If it was sent to the USA, it could be back in around six weeks' time. He was pleased for him and said he couldn't wait to hear about the results. Then, of course, he updated his father on how his own boys were doing as they were grown men by now.

Danny was an area manager for Home Bargains for the whole of Essex and Jamie had become a trained electrician, so it was great to see they were both doing well, both had girlfriends and their own houses nearby in Colchester. Terry's former wife Ellen and her brother Tommy lived there too. Steven and his wife were now living in Leavenheath and he told Terry that he was about to retire from TFL London Underground where he had worked since leaving school and that he was selling his house and buying a six-bedroomed house in Wivenhoe in Essex. Terry was shown a picture of his house. Stephen had re-trained as a chartered engineer, and was now an assessor for companies all around the country. What an achievement.

Before they returned home to Dumfries, a party was had at Mandy's house. All the family came together for photos and recalled their happy wedding. They did not have a honeymoon, so this helped make up for it. Terry was pleased that he took so many photos so he could recall the day time and time again.

25

The DNA results

When back in Dumfries, Terry received a message that Per would like Terry and Sheila to come to his house, in Kilmaurs. He had some news, but that's all he said.

Terry and Barbara drove up to Sheila's and the next day went round to hear what Per had to say. Per welcomed them in, then he told them that he had some amazing news. It was DNA news.

He told them he had a friend called Michelle Leonard who he considered to be one of the top genealogists in Scotland. She and her team were going to work on their case, but first, he told them that regretfully they had been going down the wrong road. What they had found in Ireland was not the family they were looking for. DNA had showed that there were possibly up to 77 cousins and that three of them were 1st, 2nd or 3rd cousins. One of these cousins used was Bigvic24 (the name given to protect this particular person's identity) and that would help to find out a lot more. Now Terry naturally did not understand the terminology of the words used for the connections to Bigvic24. It was explained he could be a living cousin to others and possibly have cousins too.

It now appeared that Bridget Brennan was indeed English

and not Irish at all and had, in fact, been born in England. The search results revealed that she had had nine children! All were born in England. This was truly remarkable news as they really thought that Ireland was where the family had come from. The chart that showed both of them their centimorgans (a unit of measure for the frequency of genetic recombination) indicated Terry was English on his father's side and Sheila's father was Italian but they both had the same mother. Per told them that a lot more was to come, and that he and Michelle would continue to work on it and that they were both to expect some surprises.

Bridget had her first listed child Esther Podro in 1921 who died as an infant. Then came David Joseph Podro 1922, Anita Podro 1924, Jack Podro 1926, Daniel Brennan 1928, Patrick Brennan 1930, Sheila Stella Brennan 1937 who died an infant, Terence Brennan 1939, and Sheila Joan Brennan 1942 (my sister). None of the children who went to orphanages appear to have had any contact with their parents after they left the parental home.

Sheila Joan Brennan's certificate showed her parents were Bridget and Thomas Patrick Brennan. This was supported by the baptism certificates of both Terry and Sheila. However, a note given to Terry from the LCC from Mrs. Winters gave Bridget's birth date as 6th March 1902. Furthermore, according to the note, Bridget and Patrick were married in St Peter's church in Kilkenny on 24th September 1928. Neither the birth certificate nor the marriage certificate was found to confirm this, despite the search on their two trips to Ireland. But it was known that Bridget lived in the Caledonian Road in London. She had lived in a room there. This made Mrs. Winter's previous statement untrue.

Felix Podro had married Bridget Ann Brennan neé Warren and had had four children, but from then on all of Bridget's children had different fathers. Anita Bassick (nee Podro) had a daughter Margaret Bassick, who was found to be living in Enfield. When Bridget married Felix, she was known as Bridget Ann Warren but she changed her name to Ann Brennan, and we do not know if she was married again. She then went on to have five more children, as previously mentioned. Daniel's daughter Teresa and Patrick's daughter Deborah would be Terry's real nieces.

Here's the picture of Daniel and his wife, Theresa's parents. Theresa is in the second picture.

Terry also notes that Bridget was born in Wapping, East London and her date of birth was 1898 and not 1902. So thanks to Bigvic24 and DNA, all this had come to light. Sheila and Terry were amazed at all this and waited for any more news that Per and Michelle might bring. It was not long in forthcoming.

Felix and Ann Podro married in 1920 and split between 1926 and 1928. She married the new man in her life, Thomas James Brennan but he then left her and married a woman called Fanny Natalski in 1935 and when she died in 1960, Thomas once again married this time to a Karola Greenboum. To their knowledge, perhaps not surprisingly, he had no children with his 2nd and 3rd wives. At present, they do not know the location or the date of Thomas's birth or death, but there is a distinct possibility that he was the father of Daniel Brennan. The father of Sheila Stella Brennan is still unknown. Terry's father is still unknown, but Sheila's paternal side of the family shows strong links to Italy as several of those share DNA with connections in the vicinity of Pordenone.

Per had contacted Margaret Conza (Bassick) and Deborah, (whose father was Patrick O'Brien) who are all in the London area, and with Teresa (whose father was Daniel Brennan) who lives in Whitstable in Kent. They have all confirmed what Per and Michele had traced from DNA searches and they are their nieces. Terry and Sheila have contacted them and plan to meet and share our news. Teresa has done research herself and so has Deborah (Debby) and we are in constant touch with Per so they can put things together for us. Bridget had a complicated life. She must have had it hard in those days of the war, when Terry was born and of course, it was tough for everyone. He has strong feelings for her and what she must have gone through. Mrs. Winters was the same when he saw her before she died and with nine children of her own. But as far as he knew they all had the same father, and if she lived in the same house, he didn't know how she would have coped. All that we now know was because Sheila had met Per and Ann and Per had heard our story from all we tried to find out in Ireland.

26

Trips to London

Terry and Barbara went down to London for a break. It was also her 85th birthday and Mandy and Charlie had planned a night out at Boisdale Restaurant in Belgravia. It was the most expensive they had ever been to. The entertainment was a Rat Pack tribute, featuring artists such as Frank Sinatra and Dean Martin. They all thought they looked and sounded like the real thing! And as it was Barbara's birthday, they sang a tune dedicated to her. She loved that experience and everyone enjoyed the meal. Charlie paid for it and they thanked him for the special evening.

Terry went up to Wivenhoe to see Stephen's new house. It was huge with spacious rooms to sit in, but they sat in the back garden with his wife Julie and had long chats about family and things and about their children Danny and Jamie, but Terry was disappointed not to see them on this occasion. Stephen took them to a local pub for lunch on the riverside, a short walk from his house. On the walls in his home were the certificates of his work and his chartered engineering awards sitting along with his award for 25 years with TFL Underground. Terry had a wonderful day before he took the train back to London.

Terry went to St. Charles Borromeo in Warren Street as this was where Daniel Brennan was baptized just to feel that he'd been there. It was closed. But as he was about to walk away, a lady came out of a side door. He asked if he could have five minutes inside and explained why. There was a Polish man sitting there and she was trying to get him outside. He would not move. Terry was disappointed with what he saw so he left the woman and her problem Pole!

He always wanted to walk along the south side of the Thames from St Paul's to Westminster and visit St Paul's. He went inside and wanted to get to the whispering gallery, but the lift was out of action. However, the priest pointed to the stairs, so he started to climb and after 375 steps he felt his knees and wondered if he was near the top but there were in fact another 150 to go. He gave up and returned to solid ground. He crossed the London Millenium bridge and started to walk along, and as he went, he saw all the sights of London along the way and must say he really enjoyed them. Although he had lived there for many years, he had never taken the time to see that part of London. Naturally, Terry went to the cemetery to see Bridget's grave and this time after tidying up, he left some artificial flowers which would bloom longer than cut flowers.

Mandy had booked a Karaoke Bingo and Burlesque night out for them. This works by having a number called out and then a song played to match the number. It seemed so funny how it worked but the prizes were worth mentioning. A double freezer, a TV and a boat were on offer. The Burlesque part of night continued, and the acts circulated around the tables. It was such a fun night and although they didn't win nothing, it was a good way to end this evening in good company.

On another trip, Terry went to Victoria Station, walked along Westminster Bridge on the south side and walked back the other way. As he walked, he came across the OXO building and nearby on a bench he saw a wallet. No one was sitting beside it. He looked inside and found it had £60, an ID card and the rest was all in German. Apparently, it belonged to a fourteen-year-old German girl with an address for Germany inside, so he took £10 out of it and used it to post it back to her. It was collected and signed for, but he never got a thank you answer back. It seems that you don't always receive thanks for some good deeds.

27

Meeting the Nieces

Per had been in touch with all three people whom they now could call nieces and Terry made a date to travel to the Barbican Centre to meet Teresa who lives in Whitstable. They had lunch together and for the very first time he met a living relative other than his sister, Sheila.

There was much to talk about, but Teresa was clued up about her family. She had a mother and brother in Surrey, her father was Daniel Brennan who would have been Terry and Sheila's brother. As they spoke about him, Terry learned that he was also sent to an orphanage at the age of 7 years. It was to St. Dominics Priory Convent school in Hertfordshire, that he was sent. Bridget had sent him pens and paper for him to write to her but apparently, he never answered her.

At that time Bridget was living at 76 Cleveland Street, London W1. Bridget's name, at that time, was O'Brien. The father was listed as Thomas Brennan. It had been confirmed they lived at this address.

On March 9th, 1947, Daniel was working for a family called Conti at their restaurant. In 1949 Daniel moved to 240 Liverpool Road, N1 and Daniel began to renovate the house. In 1950 he married Maria Concetta. He was employed at Fetter Lane, EC1 and remained living in Liverpool Road during his working life. He died on 7th June 2003 at a new residence at 93 Days Lane, Sidcup, Kent. His whole life, Daniel thought he was an orphan and illegitimate not having had any contact with his parents. He knew his parents' names; he even knew his date of birth but not the place. He also thought he was Irish like Terry and Sheila, and due to his circumstances, he had hoped to be sent to Australia like many of his generation were. Worse of all he had suffered sexual abuse in the convent and had witnessed his father being violent towards his mother before being placed in the orphanage. Ironically, Daniel lived in Caledonia Road for a short while at number 513. Yet he never had any connection with Bridget. He was there after Bridget had died but it appears he stayed with an Italian woman around 1945/46, just doors away from where his mother and siblings lived. He never found out who his parents were, and it is possible that his birth was not even registered. The next time Teresa and Terry agreed to meet it would be at Whitstable, where Teresa lives. They did meet again in London but this time with Neil and Mario too.

Terry then contacted Margaret Conza (Bassick) who lived at Enfield Lock in North London. When he got there, he found that they lived in a converted shop as it were, on Malvern Road. He was made most welcome. Her husband's name was Guiseppantino and her son and daughter, Anita and Victorio (Bigvic24) were also there. Margaret made a lovely dinner and Terry told them all that he had learned from Per's papers that he had brought with him.

Anita Senior's mother was Bridget Anne Warren, and her father was Felix Podro. They had four children Esther, David, Anita, and Jack. There was never any information about Jack Pedro, but young Anita can remember her grandfather was an Opera singer and she can remember hearing him sing and she knew he was good. Margaret's parents were the owners of the shop, named British and Continental Stores, and had lived there until they died. Margaret too was the owner of the shop. We talked for hours, and they began to call me Uncle Terry. They said they'd love to meet Sheila, so next time he told them he'd bring her with him.

Terry and Debbie

When the next time came, Sheila stayed with Neil at Fulham, and they arranged to meet Debby. So, I called Stephen and Neil, Mario and Boyd and we met at Liverpool station. We went to a local pub and waited for Debby to come. When she arrived and the family together, Terry gave Debby a copy of our family tree and recalled a few things. Debby's father was Patrick Brennan and married Bridget in 1955 and had two children Debby and Russell born in 1958. Patrick left her mother again and married once more. Her brother and Debby didn't have any contact with their father but reunited with him before he died and that was when.

Debbie discovered they had a half-brother born from the second marriage. There was confusion about her father. He was born possibly in Manchester in the early 1930s, but she could not confirm this. She understood her father went to school in Cambridgeshire, although no record of this exists and there was a suggestion that the people who brought him up were not his parents. This we found amazing. The plot thickens with Bridget.

Patrick lived in a house called Rose Cottage in Cambridge but little else is known about him. We left Debbie to get her train back home and we all said we'd like to meet again sometime.

28

Back in Dumfries

Saturday nights were the nights when Terry and Barbara got dressed up and went to the local R.A.F. club in town. All the time they went there they would meet friends from Dumfries, danced and socialized. Each year they had a meeting to elect new members to the committee and they were looking for a treasurer. So, Terry volunteered. The club was in debt to the brewery and bills were not being paid on time. Terry took it in hand and opened a big ledger book with strict control of the finances, getting rid of unnecessary stuff that they had.

Once the financial affairs had started to look better, as Terry had managed to get them out of debt, the staff could be paid holiday money as they had not had any before. His thoughts were to try and make extra money for the club, so he devised a game and the members seemed keen on playing it. The game consisted of ninety numbers at a pound a number. Whoever secured the last number got £60 and the club £30 so it was a fun for all and a good earner for the club. But despite Terry's efforts, as time went on, they had to call an extraordinary meeting of members.

Terry sent out warning letters to all to attend, but hardly anyone turned up, in fact only one member did.

It was time for the committee to inform members that the club would close with immediate effect as the long-term financial outlook was still not good. And on the last night, guess what? The club was packed to the gunnels. Someone had told them the drinks were free. There was no free drink plan, of course, but that night they took more money than they had taken for months. After the club closed, the assets needed to be sold including a full-sized snooker table, glasses and drink stock. When all this was done. The club had enough money to pay the staff the redundancy they were due. Whenever he is in town and meets a former member, they say they really miss the club as there is nowhere else to go now. He tells them he is sorry and that it affects him too, but it was entirely down to members not supporting the club.

Barbara and Terry used to go to places like Morecambe and Blackpool for weekends to stay in hotels but no longer. They consider family comes first and that means trips to London. It all costs money and it's expensive in the seaside towns now. They occasionally go to Glasgow on free bus passes, but it's 2 hours there and back so it's a full day. Terry no longer goes fishing and has sold all of his fishing gear, although he was sorry to see it go. As with most things these days, it's getting too expensive and the new committee has ruined the club in many ways. But he did enjoy the peace and calm of the sport.

He really likes living in Dumfries as it is generally a quieter place and as they are only 5 minutes away from the countryside and wooded areas this really adds to the calmness. They have good neighbours like Bernard Heggarty who put him in touch with the prolific author Miller Caldwell who is Ghost writing this book for me.

Terry considers life to be much better now. Carlisle is only a short drive away, so he leaves his car with his friend George, who drives them to the station and collects them on their return from London. He's a good friend with a lovely wife and as he is a car mechanic, so he services his car when he is away!

29

Another Trip to London

Per eventually texted Terry more information about their search. He had found out who his father was as well as Sheila's. Terry's Father was one of three brothers called George Henry Palmer, Charles Thomas Palmer, and Henry John Palmer born in 1900, 1903, and 1906 respectively. George had a daughter called Barrett by marriage. Mrs. Winter's maiden name was indeed Barrett before marrying and she had a brother called Tommy. It might well be that as Terry said, when a man came to see him at the orphanage and he didn't know who he was, that this was Tommy Barrett. Sheila's father was Italian. His name was Di, Bernardo. It was true he was from Pordenone in northern Italy.

Per has confirmed that Terry's father was George Henry Palmer, who lived in the Warren Street area of London and that the Barrett family were all street traders with vegetable stalls and sold goods around Chancery Lane in the city. So now, as he doesn't have a birth certificate to prove who his father was, who knows, he could well have been called Palmer. So Mrs. Winters, if she were living today, would have a lot to answer for. But God love her, she did make him welcome into her family and allowed him to stay with Mary and Charlie and gave Terry a springboard to start out in life, and as we have learned, from then on things got better for him and Sheila.

So, Sheila and Terry have a closure to the mystery of Bridget Brennan who changed her name so many times and left them a huge problem to untangle who they are and where they came from. It feels great to him that when he tells people about it all, it amazes them to hear the story. His son Stephen has copies of all they have got, and he has been kept up to date with all they have kept. John and Neil are up to date too.

So, on his next trip with Sheila to London, he made a date to meet up with Teresa. Sheila, Boyd, Mario, and Terry went to Teresa whose house had a lot of renovation with a new fitted kitchen taking place. It is not surprising that Teresa was in the building trade when she was younger!

They walked along the front with Teresa and passed all the beach huts and oyster sheds to a lovely pub and sat outside in the sun. We all had fish lunches washed down with beer. Then we walked back to Teresa's where we saw her studio where she painted objects and ornaments. Neil drove us home after a very pleasant sunny day.

Sheila and Terry traveled up to Enfield to see Margaret, Anita, and her family. It was the first time Sheila had met Margaret and Anita's daughter and her new baby. Guisepantino was there too, and he took us to his shed where he made wine and grew figs.

After a small meal, they went back to town. Neil and Mario were at a picnic in Primrose Hill Park with friends. And we joined in. After a while, spots of rain descended. Then deluges of water fell. They all raced to get cover, but the rain was so hard it soaked them through. Terry made it across the road and back to Mandy's where he took a shower and donned dry clothes. Neil and the others drove home.

Barbara, Mandy, and Terry went to the Markets in Barking, Romford, and Bethnal Green. Terry always gets caught buying a dress for Mandy, something he tries to hide but they spot him, and he pays up. Mandy is so good to us; she calls him Uncle Terry and so does all her family. We end up taking home jellied eels and they get fresh pies and mash for tea and fresh prawns from the stalls. I love it.

The pub across the road is a hive of racing and football fans. Just around the corner, Michael Palin lives, and he can be seen jogging and he always shouts out to us on his way back. Another pub is where Ruth Ellis was shot all those years ago and there's a spot where the bullet went through the wall. There are a lot of celebrities around that area, as I know when I was training to be a plumber, I met quite a few.

Hampstead Heath is at the back of Mandy's and Terry often walked around there but it is quite hilly. It's a dog's paradise but there are filmmakers for adverts, a running track for athletes, and at the very top is Kenwood House where concerts are held. We once had a candle-lit picnic one night. The concert was classical and all of Mandy's family were there. Barbara's sisters were there, and June and Joyce attended too. Everyone was sitting in groups all around the big field and the stage was in the distance, but you could hear the music very clearly.

Sadly, June and Joyce have passed away. I enjoyed meeting them. They stayed with Mandy as their carer in later years. Mandy is an experienced carer.

When in London I travel to see how Neil is getting on working on houses he buys and sells and moves to the next house. He's been doing this for years with Mario. They do some fantastic work; anything from erecting another floor of a building, installing new bathrooms and kitchens, and redesigning the gardens. They have no problem selling them as they are so well-finished. What is good is that Stephen,

John, and Neil have all been successful in life and have always worked hard on what they do so they deserve all they have got.

30

Terry's story

This autobiography of Terry's life has been on his mind since Sheila and Terry found out they had a family of their own and they treasure them all. To think he started off in an orphanage, not knowing that they were brother and sister till he was 12 years of age and not knowing they had any family was a burden. As Terry was not registered at birth it made him feel lost and alone. But as Terry says, thank God they found each other, and that they were determined to find out something of their parentage. From that one piece of paper from Mrs. Winter which she gave to Mr. Clark, it would be hard to find anything from that alone. but thankfully finding Sheila's birth certificate to match some of the information on that piece of paper was a start to go on to find more.

Terry feels that getting no help from the Winters family, who for some reason seemed to consider it all a big secret that needed to be kept is strange and he can't understand why. Perhaps it was the age that they lived in. But he really doesn't don't know. The connection with the Palmer and Barrett families is still a mystery but he suspects that the man who visited him at school was Mrs. Winter's brother, Tommy Barrett or George Palmer, and it may be why she did not wish to spill the beans about them.

Sheila and Terry have now accepted that Per and Michelle have produced the final truth about their family. They can only say a huge thank you to them both. To have completed that onerous amount of work on their behalf has left Terry and Sheila with undying sense of gratitude. Heartfelt thanks go out to both of them.

It only leaves Terry to say a big thank you to all the people he has met during his lifetime. With Barbara's family and now the newfound nieces he has made, he has something to behold. He's proud of all his achievements from bacon cutting, plumbing, running, fishing, singing, and walking the hills with his sister Sheila, having Stephen and two fantastic nephews Neil and John. So, to everyone who reads this book, he leaves this message with you. There is always hope. And NEVER GIVE UP.

Postscript

The Family Tree

This is a complicated family but with the help of time, Genealogy, DNA analysis, BigVic24, and members of the living family, they have slowly been able to develop the family tree. It's not the traditional branch tree. That would require a roll of wallpaper! Many thanks to our DNA specialist Michelle Leonard, without whose help we would never have solved the many mysteries we were confronted with.

Firstly, Sheila was born in St Mary's Hospital in Islington, London, and her birth certificate showed her home was 78 Caledonian Road, Islington. Her mother was Bridget Brennan neé O'Brien and her father's name was Thomas Partick Brennan. Shortly after giving birth, Sheila's mother was hospitalized with cancer, and she died shortly thereafter on 3rd March 1943. Sheila's father was thought to be fighting in WW2 on the African continent. Hence a friend of the family, Mrs. Winters, helped with the signing of the death certificate for Bridget and with her funeral arrangements. Sheila was sent to a children's home in March 1944 and eventually ended up in St Anne's Convent in Orpington, Kent. Six years later at St Anne's, she learned that her brother Terrance Michael Brennan was at the same orphanage.

Ever since they met up in 1950, they have been in close contact and together they have tried to find out a bit more about their family. It would take 70 years before the mystery surrounding their mother and father would be solved. This is their story. The family tree has been prepared in memory of Annie Warren, a woman who halfway through her life, changed her identity and took her secret to her grave. Little could she have known about the power of DNA and BigVic24.

This book is printed on paper from sustainable sources managed under the Forest Stewardship Council (FSC) scheme.

It has been printed in the UK to reduce transportation miles and their impact upon the environment.

For every new title that Troubador publishes, we plant a tree to offset CO_2, partnering with the More Trees scheme.

MORE TREES
LET'S PLANT A BILLION TREES

For more about how Troubador offsets its environmental impact, see www.troubador.co.uk/sustainability-and-community